A Youth Worker's
Field Guide to Parents
UNDERSTANDING PARENTS OF TEENAGERS

DANNY
KWON

FOREWORD BY WALT MUELLER

ON *A YOUTH WORKER'S FIELD GUIDE TO PARENTS* ...

Parenting well is the hardest job on the planet. Partnering with parents in youth ministry may be the second hardest job. Regardless of your level of ministry experience, Danny's personal stories and practical ideas will help you love and serve not just teenagers, but entire families.

Kara Powell, PhD I @kpowellfyi
Executive Director, Fuller Youth Institute
Fuller Theological Seminary
Co-author of *Sticky Faith*

When you reach the family, you reach the world. Danny Kwon has done an excellent job helping us learn how to partner with parents in youth ministry. His experience and expertise come across on every page. This book will motivate your team to understand that family ministry is not just a program but a mindset. This is an important book for youth workers.

Jim Burns, PhD I @drjimburns
President, HomeWord
Author of *Getting Ready for Marriage* and *Confident Parenting*

Where was Danny Kwon when I was starting out in youth ministry? I noticed something when my kids became adolescents: As a younger youth worker, I tended to think I knew better than (most) parents. Then, when my oldest hit middle school, I knew much more than any youth worker, I knew my child. Danny Kwon is both a long-term veteran of great youth ministry and a careful, self-aware parent—and *A Youth Worker's Field Guide to Parents* will help you to treat parents as partners, not as projects or obstacles. With insight and wisdom, this practical and accessible resource will help any youth worker build bridges with parents as the foundational relationship for a healthy, biblical youth ministry.

Chap Clark, PhD I @chapclark
Professor of Youth, Family, and Culture
Fuller Theological Seminary
Author of *Hurt 2.0*

When I discern what books I'll spend my limited time reading, I ask myself a couple of intrinsic questions: *Do I trust the author's authority? Is this something I need to understand more about now?* Those answers are an enthusiastic yes for Danny Kwon's inaugural book. Danny is a long-time friend and I've seen him work this out in his life and ministry. This is the perfect first book for him. He's a war-tested expert and ferocious learner. His perspective is unique and critical. His advice mixed with humility is gold. I desperately wish this book was available when I started youth ministry.

April L. Diaz | @aprilldiaz
Director of Coaching, The Youth Cartel
Youth Associate, Slingshot Group
Author of *Redefining the Role of Youth Worker*

Working with parents isn't always easy. In writing this *essential* guide to working with parents, Danny has moved the "What's the best approach to working with parents?" conversation light-years forward. I love Danny's book. It's smart. It's insightful. It's practical. The best aspect of this book is the real world connection that Danny makes to youth ministry. Danny is a practitioner—his ideas and advice are vetted in his church. This isn't a book filled with ideas that *might* work in your ministry, it's packed with effective strategies that will *absolutely work*. Read and digest this book. I'm convinced you won't find a better resource than Danny's *A Youth Worker's Field Guide to Parents*.

Tim Baker, MDiv | @ywjournal
Director of Student Ministries, Trinity Episcopal Church
Editor, *YouthWorker Journal*
Author of *The Youth Worker Book of Hope*

Danny Kwon is one of my favorite youth workers and he's the perfect person to write *A Youth Worker's Field Guide to Parents*. His introduction says it all, "I am a parent ... and a youth worker." So few make it to this point in youth ministry: being a parent of teenagers and still mixing it up in the trenches of the youth ministry world. This book honestly is a must read, and I absolutely loved it! It is full of wisdom, truth, and stories that will deeply resonate. In this book you will find a mentor and an empathetic friend. Buy it for yourself, your staff, and for all of your volunteers!

Brock Morgan | @brockmorgan
Associate Pastor of Youth Ministry, Trinity Church
Author of *Youth Ministry in a Post-Christian World*

A Youth Worker's Field Guide to Parents
Understanding Parents of Teenagers

Danny Kwon

Publisher: Mark Oestreicher
Managing Editor: Tamara Rice
Cover Design: Adam McLane
Layout: Adam McLane
Creative Director: Peter Griffin

ISBN-13: 978-1-942145-04-2
ISBN-10: 1942145047

The Youth Cartel, LLC
www.theyouthcartel.com

Email: info@theyouthcartel.com

Born in San Diego
Printed in the U.S.A.

CONTENTS

FOREWORD

"What are you going to do with parents?"

That simple question thrown at me by a seminary professor just a few days before my graduation rattled my young, late-twenty-something youth-worker self. I had taken a short hiatus from local church youth ministry to go to school. Now, I was graduating and heading back to a youth ministry position, this time in a suburban Philadelphia church. Things were about to change.

That simple prompt and the conversation that followed forced me to reboot my approach to youth ministry by taking the scriptures and God's call to parents—to assume the role of primary spiritual nurturer of children—more seriously. I had left a youth ministry job and gone off to seminary believing that I could do a better job than parents. After all, I was closer in age and much more knowledgeable (or so I thought … sadly) than their parents. Now, I was leaving seminary knowing that, as a youth worker, my clear calling was to play a secondary role in kids' lives. After repenting of my earlier arrogance, I launched into this new youth ministry position with the commitment to see myself as a support to parents as they fulfilled their God-given calling.

Those years immediately following seminary were an amazingly fruitful time of youth ministry. I believe God blessed those years by shattering my prior ego and pride in ways that allowed me to see and assume the secondary supportive role he had for me. I worked hard to understand parents and their unique needs, pressures, and challenges. I endeavored to support them by standing behind them, by connecting them with helpful resources, and by letting them know they had an advocate in me. I stopped trying to take on their roles, and

11

instead simply fulfilled my role by supporting them in theirs. While our ministry had its share of bumps and bruises—and I did make more than my share of boneheaded mistakes—our ministry was marked by a healthy and strong alliance between the home and the youth ministry.

Twenty-five years ago those commitments birthed the Center for Parent/Youth Understanding. Since then, I've been passionate about convincing youth workers that that's the way it's supposed to be. I continue to tell them, "Don't make the same early mistakes I made. You aren't there to supplant parents. You are there to support them."

Hopefully, I've learned that youth ministry wisdom comes with time, firsthand experience, and a willingness to learn from the experiences of others. I'm working hard these days to teach that reality to young youth workers, while sharing any little nuggets of wisdom that I've accumulated over my years doing this wonderful thing we call youth ministry. I've also encountered a growing number of experienced youth workers whose time and effort (and even their mistakes) have yielded some great insights and advice. We all agree … if we can help the young women and men in youth ministry do things right by sharing what we've learned from doing things both right *and* wrong, then we're actually being good stewards of our years of experience.

Danny Kwon is a long-time buddy whose experience and longevity in youth ministry have led to a growing quantity of firsthand wisdom. He picks brains. He asks questions. He's teachable. He's a parent and a youth worker who has worked with parents. He's learned from his experiences and the experiences of others. Now, he's sharing what he's learned about ministering to and with parents with the rest of us. Danny is one of the many voices of experience we need to hear.

That same seminary professor who asked me the question that forced me to change the trajectory of my youth ministry also shared these words of wisdom: "I've worked with teenagers in schools, churches, and parachurch ministry settings, and the one thing I've learned during that time is this: In terms of their faith, kids become like their parents. Ministry to and with parents is a non-negotiable."

Danny Kwon has learned that same lesson and, amazingly, he has woven these commitments in and through his long-term youth ministry at a church that is literally a stone's throw from the church in suburban Philly where I also experienced the great joy of ministering to and with parents. Together with Danny, I pray that this would become your youth ministry story as well.

God bless you on this youth ministry journey!

Walt Mueller
Center for Parent/Youth Understanding

ACKNOWLEDGMENTS

To Jesus Christ, my personal Lord and Savior. There are no words to describe the centrality of my faith in God in my life. Jesus has been my rock throughout this writing process and for my entire life. Thank you, Jesus.

To my wife, Monica. I love you. You are an amazing wife and without your support and sacrifice, I wouldn't be who I am today. You are an amazing professor and counselor of marriages and families. Every day you help me be a better parent. All of the triumphs and struggles I've experienced as a parent and as the pastor of families and youth, you've walked with me and helped me to love our own teenagers, our youth group, and our parents more effectively. Much of the intellectual thoughts in this book came from our talks in the car, or late-night conversations, or discussing and "borrowing" from the great material you use to teach others. God has blessed me so much through you. You are so humble and pure before God, and your life truly glorifies him.

To my own teenagers—Luke, Noah, and Caleb—who did not even exist in this world when I started doing youth ministry. Thank you, boys, for your sacrifice and patience. You have put up with me through many failures and hardships. Our family life has truly enabled me to be the youth and family pastor for twenty years at one church, as well being your parent and youth pastor. That must not be easy for you. Forgive me if I wasn't the loving father I should have been. I've strived to do my best and worked hard to be a model for you of what it means to give your utmost for God's purposes. I hope you will see this as a model for your lives and live to do your best for God.

To my father and mother, Hyok Su and Hong Ja Kwon, the

best parents ever. As my brother Mike and I have both stated about our father, he was the hardest-working person we've ever known and with a large and generous heart. We owe our lives, devotion to hard work, and any successes we have or will have to his lifetime of sacrifice. Emigrating from Korea to the United States, he lived the epitome of an immigrant's life. He was diagnosed with cancer a few years ago, and now he rests in his final destination in heaven—he is at peace with Jesus. But he is intimately tied to this book. I love and miss you, Dad. And, to my mother, thank you for your love and care for my brother and me. You sat with us many nights as children, checked our homework, taught us concepts we did not understand, and were very patient. You were my first teacher. You taught me about life. You taught me about being a parent. A mother's love truly never ends.

To my cousin Lisa, who served as a personal editor for this work. I could not have done it without you.

To the many youth pastor interns I've have served with and especially those who were with me during this writing process: Joshua Lee, Gieyun Kang, Peter Lee, Walton Lee, and Joseph Kim. My love for youth and family ministry has flourished while observing my fellow partners in the gospel. I hope this book will further our field of ministry and pastoral ministry in general.

To the Yuong Sang Church youth group (YSY) and Yuong Sang Church in Horsham, Pennsylvania. While I have served at a few other places during temporary transitions, I have enjoyed serving YSY and the church as a pastor for twenty years. To all the youth who've been a part of this ministry, I love you. You've made ministry so enjoyable. And you've shown me that life *after* youth group is the most important part of youth group. Similarly, as a church, Yuong Sang has been a wonderful place to serve God. As I've studied churches and youth ministries as part of my PhD studies, I believe in my heart that the youth, youth ministry, and church I serve is the best fit and calling for me. Likewise, I have learned so much from the parents of our youth.

To my senior pastor, Rev. Yong Kol Yi. One does not survive twenty years as a youth pastor in one church without a gifted servant leader who lives out and models the gospel. We don't always agree, but you have loved and supported the youth ministry and me. And that is so much more important.

To Marko and Adam of The Youth Cartel, thank you for letting me speak my heart and for giving me the opportunity to write. More importantly, you've given a voice to many people who don't always have the opportunity or platform to share—even though all of their voices need to be heard. The Youth Cartel is truly a revolution.

Finally, once again, thank you, Jesus.

INTRODUCTION
I AM A PARENT ... *AND* A YOUTH PASTOR

You just don't understand. You're not a parent of teens.
—Parent A to Youth Pastor B who doesn't have teenage children

As a young youth pastor, I hated it when parents of youth group students said this to me. It offended me greatly. It annoyed me. It made me angry. After all, I was the pastor of their teenagers, dedicated to my job, and spending countless hours serving their children. I even tried to minster to and love these parents, guiding them on their journey, and helping the church partner with them. And ultimately, I tried to help them be the best Christian parents ever!

Today, as a parent and youth pastor of three teenagers, my perspective on this has changed ... but it also *hasn't* changed. Hence, this is *not* a book about the church or youth workers changing their entire perspective on youth ministry and working with parents. Nor is it necessarily a "how to work with parents" book. In fact, I believe I was always sincere in my dedication to my job, my ministry to teenagers, and the endless hours I spent with my students. I have been and will continue to be up front about loving and ministering to parents, guiding them on their journey with their teenagers, helping the church partner with them, and enabling parents to be the best Christian parents ever. None of this has changed.

What *has* changed is my perspective on parenting and raising teens, because now I too am a parent of teenagers. Consequently, how I do youth ministry and how the church works with parents has also changed. For me, raising teenagers is the most difficult job I've had. All those thorny issues that I, as a youth pastor, face with church leadership, senior pastors, challenging parents, and other families' struggling youth is

19

nothing compared to the physical, spiritual, and mental battle of raising my own teenagers. And let me say this for the record: I have great kids, a comfort that other people attest to constantly. In addition, my wife has been a family and marriage counselor for years, providing our family with the distinct advantage of a go-to therapist right under our roof. Finally, there are five interns who work with and serve our youth group who my boys can turn to with their struggles whenever they need help from a grown-up besides mom and dad. But even with all this remarkable support, raising my teens has still been the most difficult challenge I've ever faced.

Another experience that has helped shift my perspective on youth pastors and parents is that for the past eleven years we have had a youth ministry leadership development program for seminarians, allowing them to serve in our church as youth interns—like the ones who help mentor my own teenagers—during their three to five years of seminary. Through this program, I have seen from a parent's perspective the positives and negatives of younger "youth pastors" dealing with students and especially their parents. It has forced me to think about what I hope the youth pastor, youth ministry, and church of my own teens would understand about me as a parent and what I, as a parent, would want from the youth pastor, youth ministry, and church. Similarly, it has impacted my approach to youth ministry within our church and how we connect with parents of teenagers. We can call it family ministry, intergenerational ministry, or youth and family ministry. The Orange movement has become a movement toward this model, and Fuller Youth Institute and its Sticky Faith movement have promoted a great deal of partnerships with parents of teenagers as well—all of which we have followed in our church in some way so that we are ministering to parents and not just their teens.

Because ultimately, nothing will prepare parents for raising teens, and incorporating them into the scope of our ministry can be a lifeline for many. A recent *New York Times* article stated that "raising teenagers tests the sturdiest adults, even and perhaps especially on good days."[1] As churches and youth ministries, we need to understand the complexities and difficulties of being a parent of teenagers. Frankly, I see parents of younger children or infants, and I want to laugh. I envy them. I rebuke them. (Just kidding.) I just want to tell these parents that if they think infants or young children are hard, they have *no idea* what the teen years are going to bring. (And again, I've been told I have "good" teens.)

Now, the measure of "good" for me is character. A professor of mine once said in a class on counseling teens that your character is who you are and what you do when no one is looking. He applied it to teens, noting the dichotomy of how a teenager acts when their parents are around and when they are not around. I have expounded on this idea to say to teens I minister to that how you act, respond, and carry yourself when you're in a non-structured environment (e.g., outside of school) where there are no consequences or discipline/detentions for your actions. When no authority figures are looking, that is who you truly are. This isn't a foolproof methodology to judge a teenager's character, but in my experience as a parent of teens and as a youth pastor, I get to witness adolescents when their parents aren't around, when they aren't at school, and often when they don't know I'm observing them. And these observations can tell me a lot about someone's character, but they can also tell me a lot about parenting.

Now, please note, these observations do not necessarily lead me to assume bad parenting or rotten teenagers. These observations do not necessarily imply that parents are absent or neglectful—although at times they can raise red flags that warrant my attention. However, as I do observe and work with teenagers, these observations have shown me that raising teenagers is grueling; that even the best parents cannot control

21

how their teenagers are growing and developing. So what would it mean to parents if their churches and youth ministries could acknowledge how difficult this journey they are going through really is?

Over the next chapters, my hope is that greater empathy and sympathy can be nurtured for parents in our youth ministries. My hope is that deeper and more intentional partnerships can be ignited between parents of teens and the church. My twenty-year tenure at my present church has shown me that working with parents can be taxing. However, understanding the journey of parenthood has made my ministry to parents far more effective, powerful, and joyful. Moreover, understanding them as parents who are in the midst of a difficult job, rather than offering simplistic answers to difficult issues they face in raising teenagers, has made youth ministry so much more fruitful.

It's ironic (now that I am a parent of my own teens as well as their youth pastor) that my new question when planning any mission trip, church retreat, youth group activity, midweek program, Sunday school, or youth group gathering is not "*If* I were a parent would I send my teenager?" but rather if I would, in reality, send *my own* teenager. The guesswork and the "If I were a parent …" questions are gone. Now, this may not be the best criterion for programming—nor is it the only rationale for how I shape our student ministry philosophy, how I gauge a youth group event, or how I coordinate youth group activities. However, as I have come to understand the church and youth ministry more and more from the perspective of a parent, I do think differently about how youth ministry is executed. At times, it has probably made me more cautious and prudent, but it's also made my vision broader and sharper. All the pizza and fun games are still important, but they are seen through the lens of a greater importance, perhaps as a means to an ends.

Similarly, as I'm nearing my mid-forties and twentieth year at my church (my twenty-fourth year in youth ministry), the way I see parents is very different from the way my team of seminary interns in their twenties view parents. Likewise, the way other youth pastors in their twenties want to minister to teens and the way I want my own teenagers ministered to are often at odds. This disparity isn't necessarily a negative one but, in fact, has provided the church and our youth ministry greater opportunities to meet the needs of teenagers and their parents.

Over the course of this book, my purpose is to help churches, youth workers, and even parachurch youth ministries understand the lives and hearts of parents of teenagers. I'll admit it isn't a theological treatise on parents or parenting, nor is it a thorough scientific study on parenting. I've been trained both theologically and in social science research, so I do know the insides and intersection of these two fields of study. Rather, as I continue on my own journey as a parent of three teens and a youth pastor for over twenty-four years, I wanted to share my insights about the parents of teens and what I (and perhaps other parents) wish their youth workers and churches understood about parents of teenagers. Perhaps then churches and youth ministries could work with teens and their parents more effectively, with greater hope and with greater compassion.

I can tell you from my years of youth and now family ministry, the hardest part of youth work for me has been dealing with parents in spite of my love for their teenagers. When it comes to teens, I love their passion. I love their energy. I love seeing their journey of faith and seeing that God can use me and our youth ministry to be a part of their journey. But, to be honest, working with their parents has been the most trying and difficult part of my job.

A youth pastor friend once called me a "unicorn" because I've ministered in my church for two decades. I was tickled and kind of proud of that line, because youth pastors staying in one church for that amount of time just don't exist—much like unicorns. And the truth is, while a typical youth pastor might move on from a given church in a relatively short amount of time for a lot of reasons, it's almost never about the teenagers but *is* often about the parents.

Nevertheless, while working with parents has been the toughest part of my long ministry tenure at my church, it is actually coming to understand them that has helped me persevere over the long haul. Now as a parent of teens myself, my love and compassion for the journey of parenting enables me to embrace moms and dads all the more in youth ministry. And ultimately, it serves as a means to minister and love their teenagers more, which is, after all, why I remain in youth ministry.

Finally, let me say again to be clear that while parenting my own teenagers is hard and that dealing with parents has been one of the most difficult struggles for me in doing youth ministry, *I have the deepest love and empathy for them.* Well-known comedian Jim Gaffigan once said something like this: "If you complain about how difficult something is, it's because you're trying to accomplish something that *is* difficult."

And in thinking soberly about my journey in youth ministry and working with parents, it may indeed be something difficult that I'm complaining about. I've been trying to accomplish something difficult but remarkable with the parents of teenagers in our youth ministry, which is loving their teenagers and hoping to see Jesus in their lives during and long after they leave our youth group.

CHAPTER 1
PARENTS ARE NOT (ALWAYS) THE ENEMY

*It's hard to absorb how much childhood norms have
shifted in just one generation. Actions that would have
been considered paranoid in the '70s ... are now routine.*
—Hanna Rosin

We have a very fruitful and wonderful meeting with the
seminary interns of our youth group every Wednesday. It's
a great time that starts with one of us sharing some wisdom
from Scripture then each of us sharing our life situations and
struggles in the context of prayer requests. We have come to
realize that this is one of the most precious times of our week.
It has become a time of truly spurring each other on. It is a
partnership of accountability as we strive and press on in our
struggles and daily lives.

After this ideal start we get to the "business" side of our
meeting, and sometimes this is where it can get kind of ugly.
Admittedly, I've often been the gang leader of this ugliness.
The reflection upon our students' lives isn't the ugly part. In
fact, it's a time of joy, care, and concern, as we discuss the life
situations of our students in the youth ministry. We talk about
who is struggling with what, who we need to hang out with and
visit, who we haven't seen in a while, etc.

But discussing our students naturally leads to talking about
their parents, and this is where it can go from helpful talk to
gossip to ugliness. I used to call this "work product," the term
lawyers use to describe the material collected for trial that
is discussed behind closed doors and never disclosed in the
courtroom. But perhaps our meetings and discussions could
actually be called "righteous" or "glorified" gossip, with the
primary gossip being about parents.

We share the difficulties and struggles we've had with parents. We talk about outrageous requests they've made. We vent about how parents expect us to raise their teenagers. We get angry when they don't trust the youth ministry or don't send their teenagers to youth group. Overall, it seems as if sometimes in those moments we're actually making parents the enemy.

As I was talking about this book and its title with another youth pastor friend Moses, he joked that the real issue is understanding parents who *act* like teenagers. I thought it was humorous and have to admit that sometimes it's true. Perhaps that's because we unfairly expect more from parents. We expect them to be the mature and wise adults, in particular those in the church and those who send their teenagers into our youth ministries. After all, they are actually the ones tasked with raising responsible young people who love Jesus. But why does it seem like some parents are really immature in their faith? Why aren't some of them sending their kids to youth group if they are so frustrated by their behavior? Why do some have kids who aren't even attending church at all?

We have a fantastic, large, and well-run summer mission program in our youth ministry. In fact, over a hundred students participate annually in at least one of the four summer trips, and I believe this speaks to the overwhelming interest and participation in our youth ministry. Our mission trips also highlight the valuable and important discipleship and character-building our youth ministry strongly believes in, and this has been the real fruit of these trips—which is perhaps not always evident right way, especially to parents.

Unfortunately, though our numbers still sound great, our youth ministry has actually seen a slow but steady decline in partici-pation in these mission trips. In recent years, we have seen four students drop out at the registration deadline because they had to take an SAT preparation class over the summer. Sports camps, cheerleading camps, summer academic programs, summer jobs—they have all become more prevalent, forcing our teenagers to make hard choices. Are these things evil? Are they the enemy? Are parents forcing their kids toward these activities over our missions programs? Even things like summer vacations for families have noticeably taken priority over these mission trips. It seems parents would rather spend money on vacations than mission trips for their teenagers if the choice were theirs—and, hey, vacations aren't necessarily bad things.

So, certainly the question of why summer mission trip participation is declining doesn't just have one simple answer nor is there an easy fix or a clear right or wrong. Parents don't keep their teens home from summer mission programs because they are the enemy and hate our youth ministry. *Parents are not the enemy.* They are not functioning to intentionally undermine the youth ministry.

Of course, that does happen now and then in some churches, and I've heard many stories of parents not liking the youth ministry or youth pastor and doing anything they could to get a youth pastor fired. But despite those outliers, I don't see parents in general as evil or enemies of the youth ministry and of our churches. Maybe that's because a few episodes over the twenty years I've spent at my church have helped me realize how I could and should better understand them in difficult moments.

PARENTS ARE SOMETIMES IGNORANT (SAID WITH LOVE)

I recall a few years back when about ten of my seniors were attending the same prom. They had planned a post-prom party at the house of a student who didn't attend our church and whose parents I didn't know. As I was talking to one of our youth group students, she told me that the friend who was hosting the post-prom party was collecting $25 from each person to buy alcohol. Of course I was alarmed and asked, where the parents whose house the post-prom party was planned for would be, because surely this would not be okay with them. But my youth group student said matter-of-factly that the parents would not only be home, they were cool with it. In fact, they were the ones buying the alcohol.

Now, I know this happens. But still I was really angry and concerned. Moreover, knowing the parents of the seniors who did attend our church, I was sure *their* parents would not approve. Now, please know I am not a Pharisee, my position is that the Bible only forbids drunkenness, not alcohol itself. But it also forbids breaking the law, and these students were not of legal age. My fear in that moment was that my teens would get into deeper trouble than drunkenness, though that was certainly cause for concern. I was so bewildered as to what to do, I even called my friend Walt Mueller, the president of the Center for Parent/Youth Understanding. I'd gotten to know him over the years and asked for his advice.

My emotions were going crazy that whole day after finding out about the party. I was befuddled and confused. I was angry and indignant. I wanted to go over and set these parents straight, for the sake of all parents, for the sake of my own kids (who were much younger at the time). I couldn't believe any parent would promote and give authorization for such a thing. I almost wanted to call the cops and tell *them* about these "evil" parents.

How this story ended isn't really the point. The point is that reflecting back, I was too emotional. I mean, calling the cops was my first response? I'm not sure if that would have been prudent. What made all the difference, in the end, was letting my emotions subside before confronting the issue. I stepped back and told myself, "Wow, these parents are just being naive and unwise." This made quite a change in how I ultimately dealt with the situation.

GOOD INTENTIONS CAN GO AWRY

An important question emerged during a Gordon-Conwell Seminary youth ministry discussion led by Duffy Robbins and Walt Mueller with their Doctor of Ministry students: "Why have parents shifted from a good desire to raise their children well, to turning their children into idols?" And I appreciated the question, because it reminded me that parents aren't as evil as I make them out to be. Sometimes their good intentions and desires have simply *shifted* and gone awry.

My son is a decent football player. He was defensive MVP of his team and an all-league selection. I attend every one of his games, and I love it. Because of his size, he is unlikely to be a Division I, I-AA, or even Division II recruit. On his team, however, they have had some Division I recruits. One teammate in particular was a gifted player with the size and athleticism to play football in a big way at the next level. However, what intrigued me most about my son's teammate was his father.

I'd seen his dad on the sidelines, yelling at this son and berating and cursing at him. Similarly, I'd seen his son in the middle of a game stop and look up to sidelines and yell back at his father. When I heard his father talk to other fathers like me, I heard the heart of a man who seemingly wanted the best for his son and his future. But when I saw the way he pushed and prodded his son, accosting him with verbal abuse, it was baffling and sad.

As my son's team was approaching their senior season, it was becoming clear they had a really good chance of winning their league in the coming year and making the state playoffs. However, at the end of my son's eleventh grade year, he told me this teammate would be leaving their high school for his senior year. His friend was transferring to a private school where his opportunity to be more heavily recruited would improve—missing the senior year with his current teammates altogether. I was sad upon hearing this. I was sad for my son's friend who was about to have an outstanding year, who could have helped his team to a perhaps undefeated season, and who might have even led his team to the playoffs.

But it was even more heartbreaking to learn that my son's teammate didn't in fact want to leave the school and the team for his senior year and was being forced to. It seemed rather cruel. Perhaps the teammate's father had good intentions in mind, but it seemed they had just gone awry.

This also reminds me there are vast differences in how parents view success and achievement for their teenagers. I can recall a little while ago when I posted an endorsement of a book about nurturing success and achievement in teenagers onto my Facebook page. It was not a Christian book but it was consistent with what I see as a Christian philosophy of parenting teenagers. One parent in particular noted that the book seemed "interesting" and then posted another book onto my thread about nurturing success and achievement that was quite contrary in philosophy to the book I posted, which was a clear message to me that he disagreed with what I was endorsing.

However, it was also a clear message that this parent *did* actually have good intentions and that he would raise his teenager the way he thought best. Nevertheless, I was saddened that his philosophy was not what I see as a faith-based, Christian calling to parenting. Ultimately, I never posted a response (I don't see Facebook as a place to debate important topics such as these), but I did find time to speak with him about his good intentions that I felt had gone awry.

"I KNOW WHAT'S BEST FOR MY CHILD"

Madeline Levine's book *The Price of Privilege* tells some horrifying stories of parents.[2] The parents described in this book have "under"-parented their children and given them license to live without any true accountability in their lives. These stories depict a strong sense of entitlement as well as an "I know what is best for my child" attitude. Moreover, the parents described in this book are so blind they never see or acknowledge the depravity of their own teenagers, rather they always find blame and fault in others. In doing so, they choose to absolve any fault or responsibility that might fall to themselves or their kids.

A few years ago, I visited a former seminary intern from my church who had maintained a few close relationships with some people at our church, though he'd gone on to be a youth pastor elsewhere. He and his wife remained friends with one couple in particular because his son was the same age as theirs. The sons were in middle school at the time but, to the mother still at our church, it seemed like her son was less attuned to spiritual things, more immature, and academically struggling compared to my former intern's son.

My friend started telling me how the mother from my church would call and visit them often, complaining about her son. Not realizing the connection youth ministers have, she also vented to my friend about our youth ministry and all the ways it needed to change, which really burned me up at the time. It angered me. I felt attacked. I started defending our ministry to my former intern. I started to pick apart everything the mother was saying about our youth ministry.

But I was being prideful. After I voiced my thoughts, my friend gracefully and lovingly said to me, "Danny, I know you're upset, but can't you see she just wants what's best for her son?" His statement was true, but the truth still hurt. I needed to understand that parents, in their hearts, are—more often than not—just trying to do what is best for their children.

SINFUL AND STUPID

Sometimes parents do sinful things, and sometimes parents do stupid things. I have come to understand this without any ill will or malice, because I don't want my own heart and ministry to be pervaded by discouragement and hopelessness at the brokenness we're all capable of displaying. Accepting any person for who they are has been a liberating process for me. (And my wife would be the first to tell you that she has seen both sinfulness and stupidity in my actions as a parent too.) I'm far from being perfect, and I know I act just as "sinful and stupid" as any other typical parent in their worst moments. Likewise, no matter how hard any of us tries to be a good parent, we'll always feel like we could do more. So calling any other parent's actions sinful or stupid may seem mean, but sometimes there's truth in the labels—for all of us.

Not too long ago, we had a sixth grade student whose parents divorced. We try not to judge those getting divorced in our church, because it happens. In fact, our church hired a divorced woman as a youth pastor, which was really a pivotal moment for us—a reminder that we shouldn't judge those who are divorced or anybody else based on outside circumstances or appearances. It was liberating for our students—particularly this sixth grader—to see that we would welcome a divorced youth pastor into our ministry. It demonstrated that we were an open nurturing place for our students to come as they were, and in this particular case, it helped us to reach out to this sixth grader. He felt at peace knowing we were walking with him and that an adult in our youth group was walking with him too, from a deep place of understanding.

A few months later, however, we heard about a seventh grader in our youth group whose parents were also getting divorced. We were sad to hear news like this again so soon and, of course, we felt bad for the student. We reached out to him, and he seemed to be doing fine. But not too long after, we found out the father of this seventh grader had filed for divorce because he'd been having an extramarital affair with that sixth grader's mother. I know it sounds like a great soap opera or made-for-TV drama, but it was actually happening.

I was totally ticked, with what I believe was righteous indignation. I couldn't comprehend what the parents were thinking or the consequences this affair would have on these teenagers. Likewise, I kept thinking what it must be like for these two students to see each other at youth group, and I was so angry for them. But then I had to realize that, yes, sometimes parents do stupid things. They do sinful things. I needed to accept that. I needed to show grace because of that. I needed to love parents—even these parents—despite their sins.

IT'S NOT PERSONAL (AND PARENTS ARE STILL SINFUL)

A few years back, I attended a high school graduation that conflicted with our midweek program as well as our student mission team meeting. An hour before, I had received a phone call from a parent who had informed me that her daughter would need to miss the mission team meeting because she was very sick. "Of course," I'd replied and told the mom that I would pray for her daughter. But as we were listening to the graduates' names being read, I saw this same student walk by me. She wasn't sick at home, she was yelling, screaming, and jumping up and down for joy as the names of her graduating friends were being read.

You can imagine how duped and sucker-punched I felt at that moment. It was not so much seeing the student at the graduation even though she was supposedly sick, it was knowing her mom had called me to cover for her. This was extremely discouraging. Moreover, I was disgusted by a mother who would flat-out lie and by the negative example this action set for her daughter.

While these cases are probably more the exception at our church, they do happen. When they do, I have to remember not to take things personally. It's not about me. It reminds me of the story in Matthew 21 of Jesus walking into the temple courts and seeing it being turned into a "den of robbers." His words are even more telling in his moment of indignation. Jesus says that you shall not turn "my Father's house" into a den of robbers. These words always ring in my heart, especially as I work with parents. (And, no, the point is not that parents are like moneychangers!)

I simply love the way Jesus is not upset about what the moneychangers have done to *his* house, rather he makes the incident about God the Father; it's his *Father's* house. Jesus' pure desire that all things glorify his Father in heaven is a powerful reminder to me that youth ministry has to be about glorifying the Father too … I simply cannot make everything about me. I have to understand when parents let me down that people are people, and people (thus parents) are sometimes sinful.

It's not about me.

WHEN IT'S YOUR OWN KID
For twenty years, I've served in an immigrant church context where not all of the parents speak English fluently. Because of this, I'm called to help when their teenage children are

caught in difficult situations. For example, when a son or daughter gets into some minor legal issues and the parents face a language barrier, I help them navigate the judicial system. When a student lands in trouble at school, parents often ask me to attend parent conferences with them and help translate. Or when a parent is having an issue with school administrators, I'm often called for consultation. I don't mind doing this and, in fact, I cherish it. Even for the many parents who do speak English well, they often just want to talk to me and my wife about their children's grades, college options, family lives, and social lives.

While I treasure helping parents, because our youth group is large (and I now have teenagers of my own), I have to manage my time and energy with parents and students more than I did in my early years of ministry. Working with parents is a time-consuming part of youth ministry. Youth workers, youth ministries, and the church need to realize this. As my own boys have started the process of thinking about colleges or have gotten into minor issues of their own at school, I have realized that the impact of these situations suddenly feels more significant because it's happening to my own teenagers. These struggles have a deeper and more profound meaning. They're so much more important and urgent, so much more scary and fraught with fear. And these may seem like obvious observations, but I have actually seen youth pastors without teens minimize the feelings of parents who are confronted with these struggles.

Every year, there are about thirty-five to forty seniors graduating from our youth group, and I try to attend as many graduations as possible. But, frankly speaking, it makes me extremely weary that in a two-week period, there are about fifteen to twenty graduations to potentially attend. To be honest, I often dread going. At times, I try to get there as late as possible. I have, on occasion, been so late that cars were leaving the parking lot as I was arriving. (Confessions of a veteran youth worker.)

Despite these long, drawn-out graduations with terrible speeches and hundreds of names to hear and sit through patiently in the heat of early summer—one of our high schools has over a thousand graduates per year—I relish seeing the extreme joy and elation of the parents on such happy occasions. You can see the pride gleaming from their faces. You get to see them sit and hang onto every moment of the ceremony— even its speeches. You get to see them ask for picture after picture, from different angles and various combinations of people. What you ultimately see is how much love there really is, because this is their *child*. Seeing parents through this lens helps me understand they are not the enemy. When it's your own kid, everything that happens to them is magnified. Every achievement and every conflict is infinitely more important.

THE AGE OF OVER-PARENTING

Lately we've been discovering a new vocabulary to describe how people parent. Amy Chua's book *Battle Hymn of the Tiger Mother* describes an over-parenting phenomenon known as being a *tiger mom* (though *tiger dads* abound) and attempts to shine a positive light on it.[3] But not everyone agrees, as just two years earlier, in 2009, *Time Magazine* had a cover article titled "The Case Against Over-Parenting."[4] In a similar (but slightly different) vein as *tiger parents*, the term *helicopter parents* is used to label parents who hover over their kids and over other parents as well. Building on this metaphor, Chap Clark of Fuller Seminary uses the term *stealth bomber parents* to describe parents who not only hover but swoop in and drop unexpected bombs on our youth ministry. These parents can be so detrimental to youth ministries and churches, all because of their parenting styles.

Throughout my long tenure as a youth and family pastor at my church, I've seen these types of parents in many forms. A few years ago, we held our annual winter retreat at the end of December, and while we welcome parents to come and visit, few make the trip—especially when there's lots of snow. Still, I remember one mother in particular who did make the trip up to visit. When I found out from the student that her mom came up, I asked where she was—I wanted to say hi. But the student told me her mom had only come up to make sure she was wearing her jacket outside and had then left. The next day, the mother came up yet again to make sure her other teenager, who had an injury, was using his knee brace. Again, I never saw her, but she drove two hours just to check on her kids and these issues.

I also have parents lingering all the time during the overnight "lock-in" events our youth ministry hosts. To be clear, these parents aren't volunteers, they are parents wanting to make sure their students are behaving. Likewise, I have parents come to church the morning of lock-ins all the time to make sure the students are getting a proper amount of sleep.

In the age of allergies, gluten-free diets, and other dietary restrictions, we are extremely mindful of students and parents with these concerns, but despite our efforts to accommodate individuals I have received requests from over-protective parents wanting us to offer only vegetarian items or to get rid of all ice cream at youth events. Now, I'm not trying to minimize dietary requests—particularly not life-threatening allergy issues—or even parents willing to make two-hour drives simply to make sure their children are wearing their jackets outside. Rather, I understand it's just the time we live in. Some parents over-parent and other parents just need a little grace. Those used to managing serious health issues in their kids' lives often have (understandable) trouble trusting their teenagers to take over the job.

HYPOCRITICAL PARENTS

For years, our church has encouraged an old-school Sabbath practice of not spending money on Sundays. Many of our parents are hardcore about this practice, but many of their teenagers are not. Regardless of your theological stance, maybe you can still appreciate how much conflict this results in—and how much of it comes down to the parents making things more complicated than they need to be.

For example, the parents who hold to this Sabbath practice frequently want their teens to stay home—except for church—on Sundays. But for whatever reason, they'll give their teenagers the car keys that day despite how easy it is to predict what their kids will do with them. When these same parents complain to me later that their kids are out spending money after church, I have to ask the parents why they would give their car keys to the kids on Sunday in the first place, if they can't trust them or don't want them to be out and about spending money.

There have been other times when students don't go out, but come instead to our house on a Sunday. As most teenagers are, they're usually hungry, and because my wife and I are tired, we have often ordered pizza. Parents inevitably find out and then complain to my senior pastor, but it's often these same parents I see—through their teenagers' Facebook pages—eating out on Sundays.

As if those examples weren't enough, I remember a time when one of my seminary interns went out one Sunday and saw a group of church members at another table. No big deal, right? They were all out enjoying a Sabbath meal. But then one of those same parents came and told me of the "sin" our intern was committing by being out on the Sabbath. (Yes, even though this parent was out too.)

Now that I'm an "older" youth pastor and the same age, if not older, than many parents of teens, it's in these moments I choose to speak with a little tongue-in-cheek fun but truthfulness to these parents, who can't see the logs in their own eyes. It isn't as hard as it was when I was younger and couldn't talk to them parent-to-parent. Nonetheless, it still disturbs me to witness such hypocrisy. Still, I know I just need to accept the hypocrisy rather than labeling these parents as lost causes or even evil. They're just modern-day Pharisees who need Jesus as much as the rest of us do, even if they never see their hypocrisy.

GOOD INTENTIONS AND BITTER DISAPPOINTMENTS

In Amy Tan's book *The Joy Luck Club*, one of the themes is the hopes and intentions most parents have for their children.[5] While the book is based on Asian and Confucian values, I like the notion of parents who have good hopes and intentions for their children. But these same hopes and intentions often lead to a common struggle for teenagers: feeling like disappointments to their parents. Of course disappointing a parent is an eternal struggle for any child—past adolescence, into adulthood, and beyond. Teenagers often want their parents' approval, even if they pretend not to care. Therefore, any real or even misperceived sentiment of disappointment from a parent to their teenager can be harmful.

I remember when my one of my sons was inducted into the National Honor Society. It was a proud day for us as we celebrated his accomplishment. Then later that night, I was in the supermarket getting some dessert and ran into the father of one of my son's friends. He was congratulating me on my son's achievement but was also upset that his son hadn't made it. He started to note that our teenagers had similar grades, both played football, and were both good kids. I could see the disappointment on his face, and I was actually afraid he was going to go home and scold his son because he happened to run into me. These expressions of disappointment are really devastating to teens, especially when parents compare their children to other children—in the family or outside the family.

As much as I tried to console this other father, I needed to realize that he was feeling disappointed because of his hopes and intentions for his son. This is a struggle and dilemma for nearly every parent. I believe that many parents just hope the best for their teens and have grand intentions for them, even if they have poor ways of expressing these hopes and intentions. The majority are simply not as uncaring as I perceive them to be.

CHAPTER 2
PARENTS COME IN ALL SHAPES AND SIZES

Flowers are red young man, and green leaves are green.
There's no need to see flowers any other way ...
—Harry Chapin

Many years ago, as a summer camp counselor, the guest speaker played a song for the camp called "Flowers Are Red," but I remembered the title as "So Many Colors of the Rainbow." It was a cute little song trying to convey the diversity of people in the kingdom of God. In that same way, we see a diversity of parents in our ministries. Parents come in "all shapes and sizes" and the stories in the previous chapter highlighted some of the different kinds of parents we have including *tiger parents*, *helicopter parents*, and *stealth bomber parents*.

Some parents who send their teenagers to youth group are believers, some are disciples in progress, some are legalists, and some are more prone to licentious lifestyles. Some may even be unbelievers or simply believers who are still young and need to mature in their faith. It's important to recognize the variety of parents we have and that there's not a neat, cookie-cutter way to work with all of them.

The Youth Cartel cofounder Mark Oestreicher recently noted on his blog why he loves working with middle school students, and one of the reasons was that parents are typically still involved during these early teen years of students' lives.[6] He also wrote about how many parents become less involved as teenagers grow older due to fear, exasperation, or an inability to grasp and deal with their teenagers' growing independence. It's true then that parents are not only different, but they will change in their level and style of parenting as their kids age.

Again, there are parents who are involved in youth group and their children's lives throughout their teen years, but this won't be all parents. Building off of Oestreicher's point, this disparity shows again the importance of churches and youth workers understanding the differences in parents and parenting styles.

PARENTING STYLES

Past social science research on parenting styles as well as recent studies can help us begin to understand, as youth ministries and churches, the great variety of parents we will encounter. For example, parenting styles are sometimes reflected in the amount of control or looseness a parent exhibits. Based on a spectrum of parental control, four different styles of parenting have been identified:

1. AUTHORITATIVE PARENTING
Parents are supportive and encouraging, yet at the same time, they grant some autonomy and have good levels of communication with their children.[7]

2. AUTHORITARIAN PARENTING
Parents are viewed as harsh and use more fearful ways to produce good behavior in children and teens.[8]

3. PERMISSIVE PARENTING
Parents are more responsive but maintain low levels of control. They are non-punitive and less demanding.[9]

4. NEGLIGENT PARENTING
Parents exert minimum levels of control and are largely unresponsive to their children.[10]

That's probably a lot of psychological babble to some of you, and it may seem irrelevant to youth workers and churches. But I think these categories are helpful to begin to see the subtle but vast differences in parents and parenting styles. We are going to encounter these vast differences and have to be particularly nimble in working with all kinds of parents. Many years ago, I had an intern call out a parent's behavior directly and just tell the parent that what they were doing "wasn't biblical." The audacity of this younger intern rebuking a parent with these generic but hurtful words caused immense anger, as you can well imagine. And while, in fact, there was some truth in his words, it was extremely insensitive to confront the parent in that way. The intern was unaware of the parent's situation and the parent's background, and was not in a place to speak effectively into the parent's life. (Side Note: Please never say to any parent that what they're doing is simply "not biblical." There are much clearer and more effective ways to communicate when something isn't right, even if you're basing it on a concept from Scripture.)

My wife, who is a marriage and family counselor and a professor of counseling, brought to my attention an interesting study about parenting styles. The impetus for this academic study was in response to the *New York Times* bestseller mentioned in the last chapter, *Battle Hymn of the Tiger Mother* by Amy Chua.[11] The study sought to investigate which style of parenting was most effective: *loose parenting*, *harsh parenting*, *tiger parenting*, or *supportive parenting*—just slightly different categories than the four I mentioned earlier.[12] Both parents' and teenagers' responses were researched for the study, and you can easily guess which one of these styles was shown to be the most effective and the style that I, as a youth pastor, would want to promote and nurture in families. It was, of course, supportive parenting.

When my wife and I present implications of this study to parents in our church or other churches, parents often don't want to understand the different parenting styles. What they want to figure out is simply which style of parent they are and whether or not it's a "bad" way to parent. They never want to be typecast as the tiger, loose, or harsh parent; so they ask questions about each type of parenting style. Through the questions we're asked, it has become very evident to me that parents of teenagers are a wildly diverse group of people, and the way they parent is actually a hybrid of all these parenting styles.

Parents also often start by asking very specific questions about scenarios that have come up in their families and situations they've encountered with their teenagers. When different parents offer feedback or push back on the answers my wife or I give, we can see clearly that parents do come in many shapes and sizes and there's rarely a right or wrong answer for each family.

MORE PARENTS, MORE STYLES

Another phenomenon we've probably all seen is conflict stemming from competing parenting styles within the same family. The way each respective parent was raised can have an impact on his or her parenting style. Hence, when you have two parents raising a teenager—and maybe a stepparent or two as well—there are often conflicts in parenting styles because each parent was raised and parented uniquely. Each parent may very well have noble and ideal parenting values, but when these viewpoints clash, they are often in competition with one another … hence the important and relevant phrase *competing values*.

My wife and I have seen couples where one parent was raised in a stricter household, thus wanting to give the opposite—more freedom—to their teenager. At the same time, the other partner was raised with parents who were more detached, so that parent wanted to be more hands on.

In the end, what I have come to understand is that parenting teenagers is not a science with formulas and exact calculations for dealing with our kids. Moreover, no sociological study can properly determine or explain the absolute best methods of parenting for every child and every parent. There are such vast differences between every child, which is then complicated when you throw in couples who are married and have competing parenting styles they each believe will be the best. As 1 Corinthians 12 talks about the great diversity in the body of Christ, so youth ministries and churches need to talk about and embrace the vast assortment of parents and parenting styles. We need to offer a greater level of understanding and compassion for parents. We need to recognize that each family is unique and therefore each family will have unique needs.

CHAPTER 3
PARENTING IS A STRUGGLE

I went from being a terrible father to a good one, or at least a better one. And it didn't take all that much for this to happen, only my wife falling gravely ill. Frankly, I am not sure anything less would have gotten the job done.
—Peter Chin

When it comes to parenting teens, let me be the first to confess: I am a sinner, and I need help. Again, as I've stated before, I have pretty good kids. People always compliment my wife and me on how considerate and kind our boys are when they visit or when they see my teenagers serving at church. Still, within the confines of our own home and to us as their parents, they can often seem like "monsters." They are stuck on their phones and tablets with earphones deafening every one of our conversations and seem to do the opposite of everything we ask of them, which truly makes me angry.

At times, I even lose my temper. If I'm a little more blessed on a particular day, I may find the heart to repent and see myself as one who struggles. But the number of blessed days sometimes seems far and few between.

It's important to see that the majority of parents are not simply "bad parents," but are parents who are truly struggling to do right by their kids. They are just people, and as such they're going to sin, get angry, and get tired. On top of that, the challenge of raising teenagers makes this struggle even more difficult. It's a spiritual battle that most parents don't even recognize, because they are too immersed in it to see it for what it is. Drawing from Ephesians 6, it's important for youth workers, youth ministries, and churches to understand the struggles of being a parent, especially of teens.

Many who know me would probably agree that I have a temper at times. (Okay, maybe more than "at times.") But those same people also know my wife. They know she is a super kind, gentle, loving person. Her personal traits run into her professional life as a marriage and family counselor who has helped and served many marriages and families, including our own. (In fact, I based much of this chapter on her ideas.) So let me admit the comfort, joy, and *satisfaction* it gives me to see her getting upset at our teenagers. To see her losing her temper some or raising her voice at our kids. I like it. I love it. I revel in it. When I see her express frustration and anger, it makes me feel better about myself. It tells me clearly that I'm not the only sinner in the room. And it tells me again that raising teens is probably the hardest endeavor for any parent—even the ones who spend their whole lives studying the best ways to do it.

WHEN THE STRUGGLE IS EVIDENT

Because some of us struggle more spectacularly than others, parents can often be seen as the worst and most evil people ever. A few years ago, I went to the home of a youth group parent and sat in her dining room talking for hours. In that time, I saw this parent make her teenage son move from practicing the piano, to practicing the clarinet, to doing homework, to reading a book outside of his homework load, and all the while refusing to let her teenager spend even a few minutes on the iPad. Yes, it was a school night; and yes, this teen needed to practice his instruments and do homework. But this parent's constant nagging and overbearing nature made me cringe. I kept thinking: *Take it easy. He's only a teenager.* This mother was the most extremely obsessive person I'd ever seen, and she couldn't stop making her son work, work, work.

Another time a student of mine was caught shoplifting. He had called me first after getting arrested, so I went down to the police station to see him, before his parents arrived. He had stolen some expensive merchandise and because of this, there was a possibility that he would be charged with a more serious crime—one that could require jail time. After spending some time with him, I kept thinking: *Why is he being such a punk and not being remorseful?*

But something even stranger happened in the minutes that followed. The police escorted the parents into the holding room. Then, as the parents approached their son, they both lunged and pounced on him, hitting him in the face and beating him on his chest. At that moment, it became clear that the police and I needed to break things up. We needed to enforce peace or this student was going to get really hurt.

After finally breaking up this rumble, the police decided to charge the parents with assault. Talk about a strange turn of events. I went there to help a kid facing criminal charges, and by the time I left, his parents were facing charges as well.

Clearly, there was even more going on in that family than a difficult teenager. But in many families the root of the problem is that somewhere along the line parenting became an us vs. them struggle. It's a fight for supremacy between what the parents desire and what their children desire. We have seen this in the simplest of complaints that parents have of their teenagers. They say things like:

My kid won't listen.
My son constantly rebels.
My daughter won't unlock her door.
My son won't come eat dinner with us.
My daughter doesn't put enough time into her homework.

The list can go on and on. And granted, these are some legitimate complaints. However, parents will make these issues a battle against their kids. A battle that is very difficult to win. A battle that only leads to frustration and anger.

That's not to say that parents should give up. They should endeavor to raise their teenagers in a godly way, to teach, admonish, correct, and rebuke them. My wife has often pointed me to the parenting wisdom found in Ephesians 6, in particular verse four, which teaches parents not to "provoke [their] children to anger" but to bring them up in the Lord. For most parents, new frustrations probably build on top of existing frustrations. We get exasperated with our teens. Then we see this verse and feel like utter failures in raising them, because we probably have gotten into fights and arguments with our teenagers. We exasperated them.

I know I have gotten my sons so upset with me at times. I know it has hurt them, but it's also made me feel defeated. Within this, I think that youth workers and churches need to see the struggle, pain, and difficulty it is for parents to raise teenagers. We often provoke our teens so much that at their developmental stage, they do talk back, rebel, fight back (hopefully only verbally).

WHAT CAN WE DO?

In understanding the parents of teenagers with such deep struggles, my wife has helped them see the most liberating and hopeful news. This news lovingly challenges parents to a different mind-set and spiritual disposition in working and raising their teens, despite the struggle. As a counselor, this news is something my wife offers others as we work with parents all the time. Youth workers, youth ministries, and churches need to help parents understand this new outlook too. So, what is it?

In Ephesians 6, within the context of chapter 6 and the whole of Ephesians, the apostle Paul is talking about various relationships such as husband and wives, masters and slaves, and parents and their children. He moves to connect Ephesians 6:10-12 to these relationships to talk about how our battle isn't against flesh and blood but against spiritual realities. Hence, what we encourage parents to do is see the spiritual war that is going on within themselves first, as they raise and struggle with their teenagers. (Boom!) It's not their teenagers they're fighting; their teenagers are not the enemy. They are fighting spiritual battles in their own hearts. And let me (and my wife) attest to the truth that this understanding can make all the difference for parents. They no longer see their teens as the instigators, the evil, and the bad in their lives. It renews an affection and compassion for their teens just to see them as their children and not the enemy.

Sure, teenagers make us angry. My teens tick me off all the time. They cause me to say and do things I don't want to. I have admittedly cursed at them. I have said things I regret. My anger has caused them to get angry. Within this struggle, how can I, as a parent, first see what is going on within me? Why am I angry? Is my anger sinful? Is it overboard? Likewise, why am I getting irate again and again? Why am I doing these things that I don't want to? Why am I saying things that are so harsh when I know I'm wrong?

I'm not advocating for a loose parenting style. I'm not saying we should abdicate our roles as parents. We, the parents, need to accept our roles with a different spiritual and mental mind-set, especially acknowledging the struggles we all have as parents.

From a parenting perspective, in understanding and working with parents of teens, it has begun to make all the difference in their lives. It has helped them be reflective. It has helped them be introspective. It has helped them to see their teens in a fresh light. As churches and youth workers see the struggles of parents through this perspective, they can begin coaching and equipping them to deepen their relationships with their teens— not only for the betterment and growth of parents themselves as strugglers who are redeemed by God, but also for the spiritual lives of their (*our*) teenagers.

CHAPTER 4
PARENTS HAVE DEEP FEARS

Fear is a kind of parenting fungus: invisible, insidious,
perfectly designed to decompose your peace of mind.
—Nancy Gibbs

Fear of the potential problems that will arise in teenagers' lives can be great for a parent. Just in trying to teach my oldest son how to drive, I've had to recognize how much I worry when I think how we'll eventually allow him out on the road on his own. In some extreme cases, this sort of worry can be suffocating. My mother-in-law lost a child in a drowning incident, and I can't even begin to imagine how devastating it must have been. She is now a missionary overseas with my father-in-law and, over the years, we have been able to take some short-term mission teams to their mission field. We love going over to serve their communities with them as well as visit them in the process, and most of our mission trips finish with a day or two of relaxation.

A few years ago, because of how warm it was in their location, we asked if we could find a place to go swimming. You can imagine the fear in my mother-in-law's eyes, seeing a team of twenty teens swimming in a lake. She wouldn't stop staring at us swimming, yelling not to go out too far, and telling us after only ten minutes that we'd been swimming too long. She was so scared of what could happen to our students, because she had experienced a fear becoming reality.

It's an extreme example that hopefully few of us will ever know personally, but the truth is almost every parent lives with fears. Fear of tragedy, fear of the future, and even simply fear of what our teenagers are doing in private or with their friends when we aren't looking or aren't there to stop them.

I love reading The Youth Cartel cofounder Adam McLane's blog, and one of his recent posts discussed social media and the sentiment of many parents who often think: *If it's private, it must be bad, right?*[13] Even with my teenage boys who seem to be "good kids," I'm often curious about what they do on social media. Like many parents, I can imagine teenagers being up to no good when we can't listen in or see with our own eyes, so it's comforting to hear them scream at friends playing games like League of Legends and know exactly what they're doing.

Parents are also bombarded on Facebook with contrary and confusing information. For example, a father of a teen at my church told me he read an interesting article that came up on his Facebook newsfeed citing a study done by the Centers for Disease Control and Prevention (CDC).[14] According to this article, the current generation of teenagers is the best in history because the teenage birthrate is at an all-time low; fewer teens are having unprotected sex; high school seniors are drinking and smoking less and barely using cocaine; and instead they are exercising more. Good news, right?

A few weeks later, this same father came to me, terrified after seeing a different Facebook story about a fourteen-year-old girl who got deeper and deeper into the world of drugs from a young age, only to succumb to her meth addiction. For this father, he connected this girl's spiral into drug abuse with his own thirteen-year-old teenager; and he was sure his own teen was going to turn out like that in a year.

Frankly, my first thought was: *Too much Facebook, dude.* My immediate second thought, however, was that parents often just don't know what their kids are capable of. Their fears and imaginations can drive them crazy. Adam McLane explains that when it comes to social media, he likes to "take stuff out of the parents' imagination."[15] Well, let me tell you as a parent and as a family pastor for many years, there's a lot of stuff in my imagination. C. S. Lewis once said:

> There are two equal and opposite errors into which our
> race can fall about the devils. One is to disbelieve in their
> existence. The other is to believe, and to feel an excessive
> and unhealthy interest in them. They themselves are
> equally pleased by both errors and hail a materialist or a
> magician with the same delight.[16]

I think many parents have an excessive and unhealthy interest
in certain "devils," as C. S. Lewis put it. Understanding and
responding to them accordingly can enable our churches and
youth ministries to work and serve parents and their teens more
effectively.

Because while there's a biblical mandate for parents to parent
well, parents often don't know how or what to do in numerous
situations related to teens. It may be inadvertent sometimes. We
think we know, but we often don't. As a parent and as a youth
worker working with parents, I have outlined some of the
things I've observed that I believe many parents are probably
embarrassed to admit they worry over, but know little about.
These things make our imaginations and fears go wild. They
are subjects that parents need more help with and equipping
in, and these are areas where I believe youth ministries can
support parents more deeply.

SANCTIFICATION AND SPIRITUAL MATURITY

Parents often come to me and ask, "How is my son/daughter
doing?" They want a spiritual assessment of their teenagers.
I also see they sometimes need coaching and help to know
how to help their teenagers grow in faith. This is a reality that
continually needs to be reinforced with my youth workers and
volunteers, as I want and need to equip these parents. Unfortu-

nately, when I ask parents about their teenagers or how they themselves are doing—or mention how hard parenting is—they often don't say much initially. However, I know deep down inside they have things they want to share but for some reason don't in the moment.

Recently, I noticed a pastor online using a Puritan prayer guide as a model for parents' prayers for their teenagers. I not only had a tough time deciphering the old English language used by the Puritans but also understanding how to apply the prayers to my own teenagers. Using this pastor's suggestions, helping one's teenagers grow in spiritual maturity practically required learning another language just to know how to pray. But often even for parents who have a solid walk in their faith, knowing how to nurture the faith of their own teenagers and making faith applicable to their teenagers' lives can be a daunting undertaking—even if they aren't attempting to pray from a Puritan prayer guide. And I wonder how many youth ministries realize the difficulty that parents have with this, let alone the difficulty of talking about it.

FORGIVENESS AND RECONCILIATION

Christianity Today featured an article in 2014, about forgiveness between parents and children.[17] The article talked about parents being flawed and the deeper meaning of mercy between parents and children; it discussed how many parents don't know how to seek forgiveness or apologize to their children. Some of us have no idea. As a parent of teenagers, I've had the amazing opportunity to learn how to do this—possibly more often than most—because I'm married to a family and marriage counselor who understands how reconciliation works and has walked me through it.

As we work with parents, I often see that they really don't know how to do this. Some don't know how to genuinely say sorry to their teenagers if they have wronged them, not understanding that the very act of saying it might promote a genuine reconciliation that could lead to the future nurture and growth of their relationships with their teenagers. On the other side of that coin, others may seek forgiveness from their teenagers only with a hidden agenda to manipulate some kind of response or good will from their teens. Their apologies are often driven as a means to an end, and teens can sniff this out quite quickly. In both cases, the parents and teenagers are missing out on true reconciliation.

DRUGS AND ALCOHOL

I believe there isn't rampant drug or alcohol use in our youth group—or at least that's my hope. But I can't be 100 percent sure. The story I shared about the post-prom incident earlier was not shocking, but it was disheartening to learn that parents (outside our youth group anyway) would willingly supply alcohol to students.

I have seen parents become curious about a teenager's potential drug use, especially when that teenager turns lazy, rebellious, or their schoolwork starts slipping. Parents are typically not sure what to do or how to handle it when the suspicions arise. They often don't know which professionals to turn to or even where to go for help.

I can remember one parent who came to me long after he randomly sought the help of a drug rehab clinic. The father's suspicion of his son had become so intense that he started consulting a second teenage drug clinic, who gave him wild ideas about how to prove his son was a drug addict. He was told if his son drank a lot of orange juice, he was a drug addict. He was even told to check the outside spigots (faucets) around his home because they were—so he was told—prime places to hide drug paraphernalia. Another thing he was told was to take his teen for a long three-plus hour drive and stay silent until his teenager started speaking—the idea being that the teenager would eventually confess any drug issue if confined in silence for that long.

I may have to do more research on teenage drug addiction, but I've never heard of such ideas. Furthermore, they seemed outrageous to me. Eventually, the father forced this son to get a drug test. Not surprisingly, the son never trusted his father again. While this story is extreme, I can tell you that parents of teenagers have uncontrollable and fearful imaginations. If they suspect their kids are doing drugs or abusing alcohol, things can spiral to weird levels.

TECHNOLOGY AND SOCIAL MEDIA

The increased use and presence of technology and social media is a huge issue that many parents grapple with and have no idea what to do about. Even for me as a youth pastor, I don't handle certain technology well—or at least I can admit that I struggle with it. Thankfully, I'm not alone. I recently read an article about the dilemmas parents have with properly using technology at home. Even for parents, disconnecting from technology at home is a huge issue. The amount of literature related to parents needing to disconnect from their tech devices for the benefit of their relationships with their teenagers is vast. Some parents don't know how to do this, some parents don't know the detrimental effect of not doing this, and some parents don't know how beneficial it would be to use less technology while they are with their teenagers.

Similarly, many parents don't know what to do about their teenagers' use of technology. In our home, we decided that no devices can be used by anyone, including the parents, during our family meals. But because of schedules and competing deadlines, sometimes our entire family is not together for meals. So our teenagers have asked if they can use their iPads for these certain situations. Other times, we may just sit down for a late night snack or, in the summer, a casual morning brunch. Since it's not an "official" meal but a "snack time" (according to them), our kids ask if they can use our devices. Because they know I enjoy reading online and drinking coffee, they often cleverly add that I can also use my iPad too.

It's challenging to develop hard fast rules. It's also difficult to regulate them. I know we have some rules at our home like no computer games or Xbox on weeknights, and my kids aren't allowed to play computer games past 11:00 p.m., even on weekends. But I continually find myself asking if our rules are effective or even right. To be honest, sometimes I need help like any other parent.

As far as social media goes, Adam McLane recently addressed the question of when parents should allow children to get their own accounts.[18] He mentioned the legal aspect of social media accounts, which was an angle of the discussion I had never even thought about; and he talked about issues with schools who have students use Facebook in this context and how thirteen years old is the minimum age for use. Frankly, I loved the article, because it educated me and made me even more aware of how little I (and a lot of other parents) know and understand about social media usage.

When it comes to technology in youth ministry or church, we face the dilemma of how much or even if we should allow it during youth group activities, and we're still trying to develop and amend policies regarding the use of technology on mission trips. From a parent's perspective, mom and dad want to be able to instantly connect with their kids and know what's going on when they go on a trip with the church, but even a day at school can be too long without communication. (Mark Matlock, the president of Youth Specialties, quipped once that according to school officials in his area, parents texting their teens during school hours was actually a bigger problem than teens themselves trying to text.)

I personally don't feel the need for students to have contact with their parents—or vice versa—on mission trips. Of course, this is easy for me to say when my own teenagers are almost always with me, their youth pastor dad, on the mission trips. However, when we have sent one of our own teenagers on a mission trip without me, my curiosity and worry got to me. I just missed my son tremendously. I really understood how it felt to be on the other side, but still I know there are good reasons to leave the technology behind.

Ultimately, Adam McLane says that the best thing parents can do is create an open dialogue about social media and Internet use at home. Likewise, he notes that it's shocking to see how many parents are afraid to stand up to their ten- to twelve-year-olds. He also states: "If you're afraid to stand up to a young teen about their social media usage … what are you going to do when that same teenager is sixteen?" And I agree with everything Adam is saying. These are wise words to parents. They are useful words to parents. They are prophetic. But let me say as a parent of teenagers, it's especially hard if you haven't started with these boundaries early. Teenagers are often past the point of wanting to have a dialogue about home Internet usage or submitting to parameters for them. It really can feel too late for some families, and maybe it is.

SOCIAL LIFE, SEX, DATING

We moved a few months ago, and one day our doorbell rang. I opened the door thinking it was some kind of group selling something or perhaps the Girl Scouts. But as soon as the door was fully open, this group of eighth grade girls said, "Mr. Kwon, can your son come out to play?" I was shocked. I didn't even think my son knew any girls or talked to girls.

Other times as I'm driving my teenagers somewhere, I'll hear one of my sons get a cell phone call. He'll start talking to his friend about some girl who liked him or giving his friend advice about a girl. Again, it catches me off guard sometimes to realize that my boys are growing up.

Dating, having a social life, and even having sex, are all issues surrounding our teenagers, whether they are engaging in these things or not. A year ago, some parents at our church snooped around the Facebook site of their daughter's friend and discovered some provocative posts and suggestive pictures. The father who saw all of this came to me afterward and asked if I'd seen the girl's page. This father was driven with fear that because his daughter was friends with this girl, she might have been doing the same things.

As a parent, it's frightening to think about teenagers dating and having social lives, let alone having sex. Moreover, I have come to realize that it's very difficult for parents to talk about their own teenagers—or even these loaded issues in more general terms—with their youth workers and in their churches. But we know communication between parent and child on these issues can make a difference. So, what are we doing to help parents get there as churches and youth ministries?

DOUBTS

I love the series *Friday Night Lights*. One of my favorite episodes was the one where the coach's teenage daughter battled with her faith and consequently her church attendance.[19] I think this sort of spiritual shifting and questioning can be traumatic for any parent, especially churchgoing parents. But at the end of the episode, it was incredible to see a mother embrace her teenager's struggles and tell her she didn't necessarily have to go to church if it was such a conflict.

The mother's response was extremely courageous and brave. Most parents get anxious and worried when their teenagers don't want to go to church. Moreover, I suspect that most parents wouldn't embrace the doubts of their teenagers in such a way. Most parents wouldn't be open and supportive but rather disheartened and devastated by it.

As my oldest son and I were researching colleges, I was shocked and worried when he told me he wouldn't be applying to a well known Christian college that many of my former youth group students attend. This information was hard enough; I can't imagine how I would feel if he told me he would stop going to church, even for a while.

Most parents probably have little idea how to embrace and nurture doubt in their teenagers. It's most likely a point of worry, and then blame is placed on the church and youth ministry for not "working." It also causes the imagination of a parent to run rampant, thinking about all the wrong in their kids' lives.

Ultimately, all of these examples of situations of the unknown—these doubts, fears, or other things that cause a parents' imagination to run amuck—are points of struggle. Youth workers, youth ministries, and churches need to identify what kinds of concerns parents are carrying around below the surface on a Sunday morning. It's an important starting point to recognize these things in the heart of parents, and acknowledging them and being open to them will better equip parents to deal with these things.

CHAPTER 5
PARENTS NEED (HELPFUL) TRUTHS

*As followers of Christ, we need to be willing and able
to tell the truth as our faith relates to the world and the
issues of the day. Sadly, in recent years fewer and fewer
who have been able to tell the truth, have been willing to
tell the truth. Now that we're losing our moral compass
and footing, we increasingly find ourselves in a world
were we aren't even able to tell the truth.*
—Walt Mueller

I'll say it again: Parents need help. The recipe for parenting
seems to be laid out in the Bible. However, when life gets into
the mix, it can become painfully incomprehensible and difficult
to navigate our way. Parents of teens may not often ask—or
might be afraid or even be embarrassed to ask—for help. There
are reasons for this. Yet, parents want and need people like
youth workers and churches to see their needs and struggles as
parents. Likewise, they need people to help in the process of
raising their teens. Youth ministries and churches need to see
the honest struggles of parents and respond to them with truth.

But this isn't an easy job. When I shared stories of parents not
being the enemy, I disclosed how hard it is to see and value
parents in these situations. However, in moving away from
seeing them as "enemies," I've begun to consider how our
youth ministry and church can help them. This means speaking
truth into their lives. But telling the truth to parents has to come
in many different forms, so that we can continue to build our
relationships with them and their students. Over the years, I
have realized that (when done well) parents do value youth
workers speaking truth into their lives, even when it's difficult
to do so.

CONFRONTING PARENTS: YOUTH PASTOR AS PROPHET

For our short-term mission trips—in particular when we go overseas—we have an intense meeting schedule. We prepare skits, worship, testimonies, and songs through which to share the gospel. These endeavors take time and energy to organize. Just as my son's football team needs to practice to prepare for games, preparation is vital for mission teams as well. Our mission teams plan for months, outlining the meeting schedule with parents and expressing to them our policy on meeting attendance. Parents are subsequently asked to make commitments to these mission trips by financially supporting their teenagers as they're able and ensuring their teens attend meetings as well. But even with all this, there are still piano recitals, school band events, sports, and other personal activities that always conflict with the mission meetings. When a student or parent tells me they have to miss a mission meeting because they are required to play at their school graduation or they will fail band, should I instantly throw the rules at them and tell them they'll just have to fail band?

Similarly, should I tell another parent her teen has been kicked off the mission team—for other reasons—after months have been spent raising a significant amount of money and the airline ticket has already been purchased? What about when one of our students unexpectedly makes the district championships in a sport and now has to miss a few required mission team meetings—do I challenge her parents and say it's the mission trip or district championships? These are dilemmas we face in our youth ministry, and I always need to consider the parents and how best to approach them.

Of course, they can seem like black-and-white situations or they can seem like gray areas, but whatever the case, when I need to confront a parent about an issue, I always have a strategic confrontation plan in mind. The plan outlines what grace I'm going to show the parents as well as the impact the problem at hand may have on similar issues in the future—with that student or any other student.

There was a situation with a student missing too many mission team meetings just last year, so I sat down with the parents and reminded them about our attendance policy. I told them while I wouldn't kick their teenager off the mission team, I would absolutely not let him go if it happened the next time. Sure enough, a year later, this student did sign up for a mission trip that required a lot of meetings. I sat down with the parents again and flat-out said if he missed more than the allowable meetings I wouldn't let him go. What was carefully planned, specifically discussed, and strategically explained the year before was executed with gentleness a year later. It was a way to confront a situation firmly and truthfully, while still showing grace and compassion. It may not be the method that everyone agrees with, but we were intentional and strategic about our confrontation, as well as clear with the parents.

I initiated this strategic confrontation plan idea so I could show grace to parents, provide clear direction in these difficult circumstances, and be clear about how it would impact future issues that may arise. However, this method had actually been hatched about ten years earlier in preparation for a previous mission trip where we'd struggled with students consistently missing meetings.

One of my seminarian interns had been leading that mission team, since I was going on multiple other mission trips that year and really needed to delegate some leadership to him. He'd come to me one day and said three students in particular had missed too many meetings, and he had requested a meeting with their parents. He was a young intern with less experience, but I supported him and attended these meetings together with the parents where I witnessed his confrontation style firsthand. It made parents uncomfortable, it discouraged them, it made them angry at their teenagers, it made the parents less open to discuss anything, and I worried how they would view our youth ministry—which should be seen as their partner—for years to come. What I remember most was this sentiment: *If I were one of these parents, I would never come back to church after this mission trip.* The lesson learned was that while we need to confront parents at times, we need to do it with grace, strategically thinking about the present and future.

As I've had to handle confrontations with parents wisely, I'm reminded of the story about the downfall of Jonathan Edwards, an eighteenth century theologian and pastor, who publicly condemned a few young people in a church meeting. Not surprisingly, the parents were outraged, and the unfortunate episode resulted in one very angry church and the beginning of the end for Edwards' ministry. It reminds me that even a great man of God and spiritual revivalist needed to be careful in how he confronted parents.

Ultimately, when youth workers and ministries are going to confront parents, we need to understand that some parents are going to be defensive, rude, and will reject what we say. We will only be stirring wrath rather then being productive, even if we come to them with the utmost love. However, a strategic, graceful response at least has the potential to be much more effective than putting gasoline on a fire.

Please believe me, I know many youth pastors who want to speak truth into the lives of parents, and we do need to be "prophetic" youth pastors. For example, I read articles and blog posts all the time about youth sports in relation-ship to church attendance and faith, and the truth is there is a lot to say to parents about this subject. Just google "sports," "parents," and "church" and you will see how much youth pastors and other ministry leaders have to say on the matter. Many articles will note that the church needs to help parents make sure they develop the physical and spiritual lives of their teens; the church needs to help parents and their teens balance or prioritize sports and spirituality; and the church needs to help each family by clarifying what the Bible teaches. As I read these articles, I think: *This is all true but not as easy as it sounds.* Moreover, when it comes to speaking prophetically to parents on such a topic, even the most gracious, kind, loving, compassionate youth workers may find that the message is not received well—no matter how carefully and humbly they attempt to communicate.

Let me state this a different way: In speaking with parents about touchy subjects, I know most youth pastors, youth ministries, and churches do seek to be gentle. The idea is to be soft and funny; to be great listeners before, during, and after we have offered prophetic truth. But even still, let's not forget that a prophet is not welcome in his hometown, according to Jesus. Prophets of the Old Testament were often rejected. They were speaking from the margins and sometimes this got to them. Jonah was a prophet whose anger burned against Nineveh, because he was so rejected and angry. Hence, as youth workers, let's remember that when we are prophetic in our truth-telling, we are going in and messing with a parent who loves their kids. (Maybe even too much.) Let's be realistic about the potential for a negative response.

Parents think they know what's best for their kids. These are their children, their beloved offspring. Parents can even be slaves to this parental love for their teenagers. Parents worship their teenagers and sometimes don't even know it. Speak to any local high school or middle school teacher and most will tell you how difficult it is to be teachers of teenagers often simply because those teenagers have *parents*.

Parents are so defensive about their teenagers, especially when told something they should change or do. Speaking your prophetic words to parents about their children who are so precious to them is like trying to touch Frodo's ring from *Lord of the Rings*.[20] It was Frodo's, and no matter how nice of a person Samwise Gamgee was, no one was to touch the ring.

So, be a prophet … but be ready for the backlash and negative reactions. Be ready for a response. You are speaking uncomfortable and maybe inconvenient truths into a subject so dear to parents, and this will quite often elicit strong reactions and emotions. The truth is hard and sometimes the truth hurts. When you speak truth into the life of a parent, it can expose huge feelings. It can cause parents to feel embarrassed or guilty. It can cause feelings of shame in parents. And as the church (by definition) is a gathering of people, with this shame comes guilt. Parents might feel sinful in front of you or anyone else they think might know, leading them to avoid contact with others in the church.

In the last few years, I have seen parents of our youth group leave the church due to one particular issue: divorce caused by extramarital affairs. In these cases, we try so hard to make parents still feel welcome in our church. Hence, we try to promote a hospitable environment in our youth group—not just for the kids, but for their parents as they come and go.

Still, I can remember meeting a father at his son's graduation who was usually one of the most supportive parents when it came to our youth ministry, but suddenly he didn't seem too welcoming or glad to see me. It was really curious. Then I found out a few weeks later that he'd had an extramarital affair (that I didn't even know about), and he'd left the church. In this case, I hadn't even said anything to the dad, because I didn't know. There had been no "truth-telling," yet the response was almost as if there had been. Consider then when we do speak the difficult truths into the lives of parents how they might feel. How hard will it be for them to hear these words? How guilty and "failure-like" will they feel when it's over? Will our words drive them to leave the church, perhaps even their faith?

These questions are heavy and intimidating, but I know I need to think about a parent's heart and how the parent might respond before I even consider speaking deep, hard truth into his or her life.

RESPONDING TO ANTAGONISM AND ANGER

Despite all we do as youth pastors, we will incur the wrath of an angry parent at one point or another. I remember many years ago reading a story veteran youth worker and author Doug Fields shared about an angry parent confronting him after a mission trip once; and frankly, as a youth pastor, it made me feel better about youth ministry knowing he's been yelled at by parents too.[21] I have had parents yell at me over the phone only to hang up on me. I have had parents threaten to ruin the lives of my own parents because they knew my mother and father personally. And I've been yelled at by an angry parent in front of my colleagues at church. These situations were out of my control. But when I have to deal with an angry and antagonistic parent, I've found Ken Haugk's principles on responding to antagonists very helpful, and I've used them to create the following guidelines:[22]

1. Make sure to meet a parent in a place and time that you, as the youth worker, have chosen—especially if a parent wants to meet right way. Haugk recommends finding a later time, so emotions might cool off a little.

2. Begin on time even if the parent comes early. This is, again, to let time diffuse the situation while also expressing to the parent that they need to be patient.

3. Take notes during the meeting, so you can review the conversation at the end of the meeting with the parent.

4. Finally, don't challenge parents in the moment.

In my opinion, these principles are set up to diffuse situations of emotional anger and likewise create a meeting where cooler heads can prevail. Nothing is worse than trying to talk to an angry parent. Give the parent some time and space, be clear, and don't challenge them in the moment. These actions have led to fruitful meetings with parents in our ministry.

One other note about responding to antagonists or angry parents: Please think about how you'll respond to an angry text, email, or voicemail from a parent before you get one. It's easy to read or hear something negative and quickly shoot off a response if you don't have a wise plan (or habit) in place. I've found that I need to wait twenty-four hours before responding, giving myself time to think not only about what I write but time to understand what and why the parent wrote or said what they did. I want to try to think deeply about their perspective. Likewise, in waiting, it does give the situation some time to diffuse itself, especially my own personal desires to react or defend myself or our youth ministry.

AUTHENTICITY AND APOLOGIES
When I'm wrong, I admit it. When I've wronged a student, parent, or family, I admit it. And even if it wasn't intentional or it wasn't directly my fault, but something that occurred within our youth ministry, I believe I need to sincerely take responsibility and apologize.

So always, when I've wronged a parent, I let them know. And this does more than just foster good relationships; many times it sets the tone to be able to speak truth to them later on.

I believe it's how the mind of a parent works. Your genuine authenticity and your apologies go a long way in their hearts to build trust.

Years ago while our youth group was watching a movie at a churchwide family retreat, a father of a sixth grader along with another adult came walking into the back. They were quite noisy and talkative as they were getting some extra chairs for a room they wanted to hang out in next door, and I was extremely perturbed by their rudeness. As they made a second foray into our room to get chairs while talking aloud, I exclaimed in a not-so-quiet voice, "Excuse me, we are watching a movie!"

After the movie ended, as I was dismissing our students for the night, the father and another man came into the room. It looked like one of those scenes in a movie where they were coming to beat me up. The father got right into my face and said that I was extremely rude and ignorant.

I should have and could have backed down, but I was annoyed (and young and naive). I shot back that he shouldn't have come into the room. He said I shouldn't have embarrassed him in front of the youth group and his son; and, of course, I shot back that I wouldn't have if he hadn't come into the room. He asked why I did what I did, and again I shot back, saying, "Why did you come into the room?"

This went back and forth and got pretty heated, and to this day, I know I was not technically wrong. But I realized later there was a much better way I could have handled the situation during and after the movie. Likewise, as the new pastor to this father's son, I worried my actions might have permanently impaired my ministry to him. A few weeks later, I went to look for this father at church. I could tell he wanted to avoid me and not talk to me. I could see he was moving in the opposite direction every time I moved, so that I wouldn't have a chance to talk to him. But eventually, I faced him. I made the most sincere apology I could for not handling the situation more appropriately during and after the incident, and I also admitted my pride and my sin and explained that I needed his forgiveness.

Now, I can't tell you that every situation will work out this way, but a few days later, he came and apologized to me too. Then I was able to talk to him about how adults in our church are sometimes not considerate of our teenagers. And now eleven years later and after graduating both of his sons from my youth group (and having one of his now-grown sons as a volunteer on mission trips each summer), I can tell you that this father has been one of the most supportive parents ever. Even after his sons graduated from youth group. He has been an enthusiastic advocate for our youth group and has promoted our youth group to tons of other parents in the community. As he serves on the church missions committee, he also advocates for a bigger budget for our youth group and lets our youth group take most of the extra supplies and donations for the youth group mission trips. And what I can say from all this is, with many parents, a truly authentic apology when conflict rears its head will go a long way for you and your youth ministry. It's just another way of speaking truth in love to parents.

THE IMPORTANCE OF EMPATHY

A few years ago, we had some reported bullying incidents. Bullying, I think, sometimes starts outside the church at school or on some sort of social media. Then, once begun, the bullying pervades into the social interactions at church. Students have been ridiculed or left out of social circles at school and then these same students don't want to come to church. We have also had experiences where students feel ostracized by others from our youth group because of how they look. Either way, no one wins with bullying. Whether it originated outside of church or in church, it's happening in the youth group sometimes, whether we like it or not. Being willing to see it, validate the problem of it, and meet with the parent whose student is being bullied is vital and important.

In school, one of my children read a book about a family dealing with racial issues. This caused somewhat of a stir with my son, because of some of the racial stereotypes and teasing he himself was facing at school. I remember my son and an African American friend of his were feeling hurt after reading this book. They started passing notes to each other one day about the racial stereotypes they were facing from their peers at school, but after discovering the notes, a teacher and then the school administration got involved and their intention was to suspend my son.

Now, I would never condone some of the words and thoughts my son and his friend put on paper. But I believe as two naive middle school students, they were feeling their "differentness" in a new way for the first time in their lives, especially after reading this school-assigned book. They were still coming of age and realizing that race was an issue in their lives. This sense of alienation from others was a legitimate feeling that was the fuel for their words.

When I finally got into the room with some of the school administrators, I was hoping for a healthy dialogue and perhaps some understanding and empathy. I wasn't there to blame the school for any type of racism or mistreatment of my son or his friend. I wasn't there to accuse students of racial insults or the school of perpetuating a lack of diversity awareness. These two teenagers were middle schoolers with lots of emotions and feelings and from different ethnic backgrounds than most of the students at their school, so it was not surprising that something like this had happened. But looking back, I never once got a sense of any responsibility or compassion from the school. Even a simple word of acknowledgment would have helped as the school spoke their "truth" to me about this incident. Perhaps just saying they could understand why these two boys were feeling what they were feeling in response to the school assigning a book about racial issues. Or perhaps an acknowledgment that the book could have instigated in middle school boys a feeling that they were different—any of these things would have helped me feel, as a parent, that my son was seen and heard and that my concerns were seen and heard.

If something happens at church or youth group, let parents know you acknowledge them and hear them. It doesn't have to be an apology, and we don't need to apologize for something we didn't do. But I know even an acknowledgment goes a long way and opens hearts to speak truth.

As a community church, we offer programs and services to our community. Some youth group students participate in them even though they are not official youth group events or programs. We have youth orchestra and a youth dance team that both give students chances to use their gifts and talents for God. In performing music and dance, there are varying skill levels, of course, which has led to some students feeling "less than" or incompetent. Recently, a parent had called to complain that her daughter felt like leaving the church. After meeting with the parent, I realized that this was not related to our youth group but was because of what was going on in the dance team. Her daughter felt inept as a dancer, and the leaders of the dance team seemed to be treating her in a negative way.

I knew it had nothing to do with me or our youth group. But, still, I took time to acknowledge the hurt and struggle of this student. I apologized on behalf of the church, because this dance team was part of our church programs, and like it or not,

I'm one of the people who represents "the church" to these parents. So, I helped ease the mother's hurt as well by telling a story of my son not wanting to play a sport because he didn't feel like he was as good as others. This eventually enabled the student to come back to church. I was also eventually able to speak to the mother truthfully about whether or not her daughter should remain on the dance team.

Sometimes, authentic acknowledgements and apologies can go a long way with parents, leading to opportunities to speak truth. I think the old Young Life phrase sums it up best: "Earn the right to be heard."

CHAPTER 6
PARENTS (MIGHT) MISUNDERSTAND YOUTH MINISTRY

It's your problem!
—Parent A, on the spiritual development of teenagers

You're the problem!
—Parent B, on the spiritual development of teenagers

When it comes to youth ministry, the church, and the spiritual needs of teenagers, I have boiled it all down to two schools of thought that seem to dominate what parents have to say about youth ministry in almost every church. In one corner you have the parents saying, "It's your problem." And in the other you have those saying, "You're the problem."

"IT'S YOUR PROBLEM."

As youth ministry has developed over the years, it has become a specialized ministry within the context of many churches. Similarly, youth ministry has now been called to specifically nurture and develop the spiritual needs of teenagers. Chap Clark often uses an illustration of Mickey Mouse and his ears to depict how youth ministry has become a separate extension or offshoot of most churches. Ministering to youth, guiding them spiritually, and nurturing and developing them into men and women of God has unintentionally been left to the youth group and youth workers as a branch of the church ministry and removed from the overall responsibility of the larger church whole or often even parents themselves. I call this the It's-Your-Problem youth ministry. And it's simply how youth ministry has evolved and functioned, whether intentionally or unintentionally, over the last forty years.

Almost all youth workers can relate to this, as it's often the mind-set of parents in many churches, and it isn't necessarily the fault of the church or youth ministry. As I consider the history and development of youth ministry, I believe firmly that what youth ministry has achieved gives us reasons to hold our heads up high. Youth pastors and youth volunteers have continuously demonstrated their dedication and love for teenagers in these important years of teenagers' lives. As youth workers, we sincerely want the best for these teens.

But in all this, youth ministry has somehow become the exclusive place where we are supposed to raise the teenagers spiritually and the responsibility of both the church and parents in this endeavor has been lost or misplaced. I see many parents just dropping their teens off at an It's-Your-Problem youth ministry.

The Fuller Youth Institute is growing a grassroots movement to nurture an intergenerational approach to youth ministry called Sticky Faith.[23] It's a movement to have the whole church and parents become part of a concerted team effort to raise their teenagers spiritually and pass Christianity from one generation to the next—nurturing a faith that "sticks." Brad Griffin and Kara Powell are taking this movement to many youth groups and churches, including ours.

Similarly, Chap Clark revolutionized and rocked my thinking about the traditional five-to-one ratio in youth ministry. We use this ratio in youth ministry to attempt to have at least one adult for every five teenagers on our youth group trips, at our activities, and on mission trips. But Chap argues that when it comes to overall adult involvement with kids, we actually need five significant grown-ups to be a part of each teenager's life in our churches.[24] Only then will the It's-Your-Problem mentality of raising teenagers spiritually be replaced with parents saying, "It's everyone's problem. I need your help. Walk alongside me."

Many churches and youth ministries use the phraseology "walk beside" or "walk alongside." It denotes this idea that parents are to raise their kids and youth ministries will be beside or alongside them to help them on their journey. I use this phrase all the time, and I really like it. I think it's a biblical concept. However, I've realized more and more that it's foreign to many and is the exact opposite of what most parents think when it comes to raising their teens and the purpose of youth ministry. I imagine not a lot of parents feel like they are being walked alongside in their journey with their youth ministry. What do you think? What do the parents of your youth group think?

It is tremendously hard raising teens. Parents often struggle with it. The It's-Your-Problem mind-set is very convenient and burden-freeing. It allows room to relieve some of this difficult responsibility. It's-Your-Problem can remove the guilt from parents who haven't nurtured their teenagers' faith. To work with parents more effectively, we need to be aware of this mentality and recognize why parents sometimes don't get involved.

"YOU'RE THE PROBLEM."

Contrary to the It's-Your-Problem philosophy of parents and youth ministry, when students in our youth ministry are not turning out to be spiritual giants, our youth ministry and I have often been blamed for the "failures" of these teens—with failure in this case typically measured by outward performance and other legalistic standards. "You're the problem" is the best sentiment that sums up the way these parents see their youth workers or youth pastor.

My wife is a counselor and seminary professor who teaches counseling, and she's also a small group leader in our youth ministry. Her small group at church doesn't consist of a full-blown apologetics or theology course, nor is it a seminary course. On the contrary, her focus is on students taking ownership of their faith and feeling safe enough to express their doubts and struggles. But when a particular student from her small group couldn't articulate all of her faith doctrines and theologies to her parents, the parent told me they would be teaching doctrines to their teenager over winter break, because she hadn't learned them. (*At youth group*—was the not-so-subtle implication.) Similarly, because of this she would not be attending the youth group retreat.

A former seminary professor who taught a class about counseling teenagers once said something I still hold dear: "A good youth pastor will not be popular." He continually noted that parents want their kids to turn out to be "good," alluding to the superficial definitions of the word that parents typically use. They want their teenagers to have good careers and jobs. They want them to be kind and get good grades. And they want the youth ministry to produce all of that for them. However, he noted that it isn't actually our job as youth workers to produce "good kids." Rather, our call is to help students in their adolescent journey, to help them grow and mature in faith, and to encourage them to continue in their faith. But all of those things were also meant to take place within Christian homes—not just at youth group.

Still, I often consider our responsibility when parents say, "You're the problem." I can sense what kind of blame they are trying to place on me or our youth ministry, and I try to understand what kind of mistakes they think our youth group is making. Granted, in my prideful heart I don't think we do *anything* wrong, but the reality is our youth ministry isn't perfect. I have to use these times to think through the problems parents think we have and ask: *What can we do better?*

Whether an It's-Your-Problem or You're-the-Problem mind-set, both have become valuable axioms to understand certain parents and seek to do youth ministry better in our church contexts. Both mind-sets help our youth ministry and church see that we are far from perfect and can do more in working with parents and fostering a partnership mentality.

CHAPTER 7
PARENTS (SOMETIMES) BLAME

Blame it on the rain.
—Milli Vanilli

If you grew up in the '80s like I did, you'll recognize this song and group, who were later outed for being fakes. I really liked this song, and as I reflect back, I have no idea why I liked it nor do I understand what they were suggesting. Why were they blaming the rain? What did the rain do to them? And what was actually the issue they were having?

In the same vein, when problems arise in churches and youth groups, parents often want to blame someone or something. In a *Psychology Today*, article titled "Parents Just Don't Understand," Nick Friedman noted that misconceptions are just a part of parenting.[25] Hence, parents often see their teenagers as they want to see them (good kids), and consequently they blame outside things (like youth ministries and churches) when their positive conceptions of their teenagers are tested or challenged. It can be quite arbitrary and hard to understand why they are blaming certain entities, as well as what the issues actually are in the lives of these parents.

When I think about my mother-in-law and her losing a child in a drowning accident, I consider the struggles my wife has told me her mother faced in the aftermath. My mother-in-law spent days and even months and years blaming herself, her husband, the other kids who were playing with her son that day, and the police for not responding quickly enough.

Likewise, parents respond in various and unique ways when difficult issues arise in their family lives or when a problem arises in the youth ministry, and blame is often part of that process. Recognizing the potential ways they may respond or place blame and being sensitive to them, as well as responding to them in a healthy way, makes all the difference as we work with parents.

In my second year as a youth pastor, I received a phone call from an unknown mother out of the blue. She called to ask if her daughter could attend our annual winter retreat. I was caught off guard and didn't really do any vetting of this girl or her mother. I was just excited to get as many people as possible to come to our retreat. I had some suspicions as the mother talked however, and I also wondered why a girl who'd never been to our church would want to come to our retreat.

While at student check-in the day of the retreat, I found it peculiar that two of my students who had not pre-registered for the retreat had shown up. I assumed they were registering last minute and would be attending the retreat after all. A few minutes later, this mother and her daughter showed up. The mother completed registration for her daughter, said some random things to me, and left. I didn't think much of it and just introduced myself to the girl and had her meet a few of our students.

But about twenty minutes later, the mother ran back into the church screaming, "Where is my daughter?"

Needless to say, I was confused. Once the mother calmed down a little, she told me that after leaving our registration area, she had secretly and stealthily parked her car in the back of the church parking lot, so it wouldn't be seen. With her finest spying skills, she had noticed a taxi pull into the church parking lot around back, and had immediately driven back to investigate. She then had seen her daughter and the two girls from our youth group who'd just shown up that day, get into the taxi and drive off somewhere. She explained that she'd tried to chase down the taxi but it sped away. She was frantic and worried.

Frankly, I didn't know what to do. I was an inexperienced second-year youth pastor. But I helped her call the police and the taxi company involved. I also asked an adult volunteer to remain behind and help the mother, as I needed to depart to the retreat with the rest of our group. During the four days of the retreat, I called our adult volunteer a few times to check in on what had been happening with the mother and daughter. He told me the mother filed a police report that day and left the church, and he hadn't heard from her since.

But the day we returned from the retreat, I—along with all the students and their parents—noticed two police cars in front of our offices. The cars' lights were flashing and policemen were waiting at the door of the church. As I approached them (with *all* the parents and students watching), they asked, "Are you Danny Kwon?"

I said, "Yes, I am."

Then they stated (yes, in front of all the parents and students), "You're under arrested for kidnapping," and they read me my Miranda Rights. After which, they immediately handcuffed me and took me to their police car. (By the way, did I mention that my senior pastor was also there to welcome us back from the retreat?)

Thankfully, before they could haul me away to the police station, one of our assistant pastors came running out and started shouting, "This is not kidnapping! This is not kidnapping!"

So the police hesitated, called the mother, had her come to the church, found out the true story about her daughter running away, and ended up letting me go with their apology.

I was still fired on the spot … *just kidding!* This is the church I've been at for twenty years now.

But what did I learn from all that? I learned that sometimes when a student is in trouble, parents will find someone else to blame. (Even when the teenager has given off so many red flags of trouble that a parent will hide in a parking lot to spy on them!) They often need to cast responsibility for their teenager's troubles or woes onto someone other than the teenager, because the alternative is frightening. Someone (or something) needs to be the scapegoat.

In this chapter, I've outlined some ways parents place blame when issues arise in the church and youth ministries. But, again, recognizing the potential ways parents may respond and blame, being sensitive to them, and subsequently responding to them in a healthy way makes all the difference as we work with parents.

So who or what do parents often blame?

THEY BLAME YOU

In times of certain struggles, especially when a teenager has spiritual issues, parents may want to blame you. A prime example is when a student comes to our youth group and doesn't "like" or enjoy it. Or if a student stops coming to our youth group for whatever reason. Frequently I find later that I've been blamed.

Recently a new male student was hanging out with a lot of females in our youth group. It seemed to me that many of the youth group girls realized the game he was playing. After weeks of hanging out with all these females, they all started to ignore him and gave him the cold shoulder. None of them wanted to be "played" any longer. So he stopped coming to church and youth group. Of course you can see where this is going. The student told his dad he didn't like the way youth group was running and he didn't like me. Not surprisingly, his dad didn't investigate the real reason his son didn't want to be in youth group any longer. Likewise, instead of talking to me, the father told an assistant pastor, the senior pastor, and other "power players" in the church why his son left youth group … because of Danny Kwon.

It's probably my biggest struggle as a youth and family pastor, because it often doesn't end with the parent and teenager simply leaving. It ends, even after serving two decades at my church, with me being blamed as well.

I recently heard about a youth worker who was being sued by parents in his youth group. On a ski trip, the parents had rented ski equipment including a helmet (which wasn't typically even available for rent just five years ago) for their teenaged daughter. The youth worker made sure she got all her equipment, including the helmet. But youth workers and volunteers who take their students on skiing or snowboarding trips know it's impossible to keep track of the whereabouts of every student at all times. The best we can do is make sure our contact information is with the mountain ski patrol and with our students as well. At our youth group, we also inform our students that a volunteer or adult will be at a certain place in the ski lodge all day, and many other youth groups do this as well.

As the story goes, this particular student supposedly took off her helmet because she was too hot. Unfortunately, the student subsequently fell and was injured that day. I'm not sure how significant the injury was, but I do know the student was back in school a few days later. While the fall and injury were unfortunate, the story doesn't end there.

The mom then sued the church and youth pastor for her daughter not wearing the helmet, despite the fact that it seems frivolous for the parents to have done so. But in their times of struggle, parents will often look for someone to blame. Sometimes, unfortunately, it's the youth workers and the church. I guess it's part of what we do.

THEY STILL BLAME YOU (INDIRECTLY)

Parents' passive-aggressive critiquing and blaming of me as a youth worker (or our youth ministry) through other parents, church leaders, or other pastors, has always been the most difficult for me to handle. There are times when one of our assistant pastors will visit an adult in our church, who happens to have teenagers. The parent will complain about me or the youth ministry in passing, and then the assistant pastor will come and subtly blame me and the youth ministry for this student and parent not liking the youth ministry. When I was a younger youth pastor, blame typically came straight from the source, the parents themselves. As a veteran in my church as well as youth ministry, the blame doesn't necessarily come direct from the source any longer.

Likewise, I constantly hear from youth ministry volunteers and workers about parents from youth group taking sides with a family who doesn't like the youth pastor instead of asking important questions, working to support the youth pastor and the ministry, or even simply urging the other family toward reconciliation. At times volunteers and youth workers have been called into their senior pastor's office to be told that a family is leaving the church because their teenagers didn't like the youth group and these volunteers and youth workers are all consequently blamed.

This is the nature of the blame game of youth ministry and youth workers and how some parents of teenagers function. Youth workers and youth ministries usually work under the leadership of another pastor or work with parents who have influence in the church, who often end up receiving the critique and blame about us, instead of us hearing it directly from the source. The blame hurts, but it especially hurts when those who are supposed to be our allies don't take the time to investigate the facts behind the blame and instead instantly accept it as valid.

Our youth ministry is not perfect and not all students will like it. So when I hear the blame from the source or from others, I admit to this, but I also ask those who come to me to hear my side of the story. In all this, what is still the most inconceivable to me is when parents actually leave the church altogether, but blame it on their teenagers not liking the youth ministry. There's no defense against this kind of attack. Moreover, the truth is, it's sometimes just parents wanting to find a convenient excuse to leave the church.

THEY BLAME THE YOUTH GROUP

We've talked about blaming youth workers, but sometimes it's the other teenagers within the youth ministry that get blamed. I admit, we have had "mean girls." We have had juniors disliking the freshmen. We have had sophomores thinking the middle school girls are dressing too flirtatiously. Our students sometimes have issues with each other.

We have even had Internet bullying, with groups of people posting mean things on others' Facebook pages. But not only is Facebook a danger zone for bullying, one bad post or picture by a single teenager or even a couple teenagers can lead to parents questioning the entire youth group and its "standards." Rather than confronting other parents, they frequently want to know if I, as the youth pastor, know about these postings and what I'm doing about them. One unfortunate post, and their paranoia runs wild, assuming that every person in the youth group is doing whatever they saw or read. Parents start to fear the corruption of their teenagers is inevitable but attempt to avoid it by forbidding their teens to attend youth group or spending even a moment more in the same room with these other teenagers.

At a summer mission trip signup event, I saw a student who has rarely participated in youth group suddenly come over. I never turn anyone down, and I'm always glad to see teens get involved. I asked the student, however, what he had been up to that caused him to miss the past few youth group events. He said his family was so worried about the youth group corrupting him that he stopped coming. (Of course, at that moment I kept thinking, then why are your parents sending you on a mission trip with us? Sometimes blame and logic don't make sense.)

It's very interesting to see the minds of parents and their views of the youth group. I have come to understand that many of their perspectives will inevitably have an impact on our ministry, and that the impact will not always be positive. While there are some actions that I can take regarding certain situations—like proactively involving the students and parents when there are bullying photos or words posted on Facebook— there are other instances where I cannot control or effectively change what someone who is not my child is doing outside of youth group activities. Yet still, it's easy to blame the youth group for all the troubles of the parents and their teenagers.

THEY BLAME THEMSELVES

Depending on what is going on and the context of the situation, some parents blame themselves—fairly or unfairly—for the outcome. There really are some candid parents who take responsibility for their own teenagers and do not blame others. Unfortunately at the same time, they can often be too hard on themselves. They need to know the simple truth that God can change people—both them and their teens.

If something bad happens to a teenager or the teenager becomes involved in something wrong , it's just not always the parents' fault. Early in my years at my church, we had a student in our ministry die of a terminal illness. You could see the parents just wallowing in guilt like they did something wrong. I have even had parents find out their teenager lost his virginity, and then come in for counsel with me because they felt like it was all their fault.

I feel extremely sad when I see parents in these situations of mourning or grief for lost children or simply lost hopes. I need to be thoughtful in order to pick up on instances when this is the case. I need to move away from being so paranoid that I'll be the one blamed for the situations in the lives of their teenagers. Instead, I should reach out and nurture parents in these contexts, without assuming that it will come back to bite me. Similarly, I've come to understand that even if parents are apt to get angry with me, it's often not anger that is really about me. They are looking for somewhere to release the pain and frustration of the situations with their teenagers.

It's sad but sometimes true that parents will blame themselves and eventually their own teenagers when something bad happens. And, sure, there is a degree of appropriateness to this. I'm pleased to see when parents are noble enough to look inward when situations arise. However, I also understand the dangers of it. A recent *Huffington Post* article about parenting was very relevant to youth workers and churches seeking to understand parents.[26] According to the author, one of the initial stages when issues arise with teenagers is a sense of pain and guilt within the parents. Over the years, I've gone to court with parents, as their children face minor charges like shoplifting, and it's often a shock to parents when a "good" kid does something disobedient. This initial stage of pain and guilt in the parents can lead to anger with themselves and with their teenagers.

I believe that helping parents understand they aren't in control of how things turn out with their teenagers—especially when something bad happens to their sons or daughters—is important and powerful. Alleviating the guilt from them or the anger and blame toward their teenagers only serves to help parents move toward helpful solutions and assistance for their teenagers.

One area where I've seen this is when parents recognize a mental illness in their children. Diseases like schizophrenia and social anxiety often come to light in the teenage years. When these difficult issues arise, I've seen parents blame themselves. They have even blamed their children and tried to get them to "suck it up and snap out of it." We have had to work with professionals as well as their schools to find help and solutions. But this is always best done by helping parents move away from blaming themselves and their kids.

THEY BLAME CHURCH

Years ago, there was a really wonderful teen in our youth group. However, I could see that he struggled with his relationship with his father. His father was a rather strict man, excessive in many ways, struggled in his marriage, and was not the most kind person. Whenever this student was at my house and his father came to pick him up, he wouldn't show any appreciation for us feeding his son or just taking time with him. His son would be at our house for hours doing homework, we'd feed him, and let him stay as long as he wanted. Of

94

course, we don't do ministry with students to garner a thank-you from parents. But this father seemed particularly antagonistic towards us and oblivious to our hospitality.

This same father suspected his son was doing drugs. He started calling me and accusing the church and youth group of being full of "drug lords." The father demanded his son take blood and urine drug tests. After consulting with the student, it was decided that he should take the tests to show his dad that he wasn't involved with drugs. I know this may sound risky to some, but I was sure this student was telling the truth and felt the tests were the only way to satisfy the father. After the tests came back negative, there was a small turning point in our relationship with the father. I'm not sure if he felt less antagonistic, but at least he stopped attacking me about the church. Moreover, his son was allowed to go on our overseas mission trip that summer.

In preparation for our trip, I can recall conversations with this student. They were deep, heartfelt, and difficult talks where the student often broke down in tears. The student expressed his hatred of his family life and the struggles he was having with his dad. During our mission trip overseas, I remember seeing some relief on this student's face, having somewhere to go and escape his difficult family life, serving other people with joy, and having some distance from his dad. And in the months after our trip, he was also in a good place, but as the summer turned to fall, I could slowly see him struggling again. That's when I got another phone call.

His father was complaining again, but he didn't seem to be blaming me directly. His son had been on various church summer mission trips for each of the past summers. I personally understand they are somewhat costly, but we hope that through God's grace, we will see the impact and change in the lives of our students. According to this father, he had wasted five years of money sending his son on these trips and had seen "no change" in his son. He was accusing the church and our youth mission trips of taking his money and doing little to help his son. I noticed he wasn't blaming me with his words, but he was blaming the church and youth ministry.

While the words were not spoken, I knew blaming the youth group and church actually was blaming me. There is no difference if a parent blames us directly as youth workers or as the church and youth ministry. In fact, when the parent blames the church or youth ministry, fault always cascades to a youth group volunteer or youth worker, then to a youth pastor or someone else in the church and then, even worse, to senior leadership or a ministry supervisor.

But one of my mottos that I practice ministry by is this: *Don't take criticism personally.* Blame placed on me isn't (usually) a personal attack. In this case, I needed to look beyond the father's attacks and blame of the church. I began to see his frustration and toil with his own situation, his struggle with raising his son, his difficulty with his wife over how to raise their son, and how all this was adversely affecting him.

I'm not saying we are to ignore all blame or just see it as the fault of the parent. We need to assess and evaluate how much of the blame really belongs to us. For example, a parent once blamed our youth group kids of neglecting their daughter and called it bullying, and of course all youth groups need to take bullying issues seriously. But when this parent showed me the inciting Facebook picture of her daughter's friends, it seemed like the real problem was that picture didn't include her daughter—that's what had made her daughter upset. The daughter believed these other girls were bullying her because they didn't include her in the picture or post a picture with her in it instead of the one she wasn't in.

This all sounded ridiculous to me. I was even upset, because it seemed absurd. Nevertheless, I poked around at the situation and found out there was indeed an issue with these group of girls over—what else?—a guy. This daughter and another girl in the group liked the same boy, so it had caused a rift in their relationship. The picture was the tip of the iceberg. At that point, my wife and I intervened and fostered reconciliation and peace. All this to say that the parent blaming our church actually created an opportunity for us to investigate a situation that could have turned into something worse if we hadn't intervened. Sure, some blame on the church can be misguided, but we need to understand the mind-set that leads to this blame. And sometimes involving the church—even if it's negatively at first—can end up being helpful for the family in the long run.

THEY BLAME YOUR SPOUSE/FAMILY

An easy target for the blame of disgruntled parents can also be the spouses and families of the volunteers and youth workers. As a male youth worker, my spouse has sometimes been blamed for not doing enough for the youth ministry or even not "being a role model" for the females. My own children have been blamed because they are part of the youth group. If they are seen as troublemakers in the youth group or not being friendly enough or not being good enough friends with other kids, they can be faulted. Sometimes they can be blamed for being "spoiled, entitled kids of the youth pastor." They can be accused of being favored or treated better by other volunteers. Disgruntled parents can find any reason to place blame and unfortunately, spouses and children of youth workers can be easy targets.

THEY BLAME THINGS NO ONE CAN CONTROL

I can't tell you how many parents don't send their kids to our retreats in the winter because of potential sickness. A few years ago, there was a flu bug going around. During this retreat, our students did sleep in cabins and were active in close and closed quarters, and we did have an usual amount of students go home and get sick afterward. I can't tell you how bad I felt for them. I heard lots of parents tell me how sick their teenagers got after the retreat. And they blamed the retreat center, the close-quarter cabins, and especially the flu bug that was going around that winter.

The next winter, we had about a twenty percent dip in attendance for that retreat. For a youth group of over 200, that was a significant reduction, and the cause was parents who were afraid their kids would come back sick and wouldn't be able to go to school after their winter break. Now, it's amazing how good God is because we had no one, and I mean no one, get sick during or after the retreat that following year. However, it's not all positive news because our retreat participation is still feeling the residual effects of that situation a few years later. Parents often simply blame random things like nature, which youth ministries cannot control, and it might just affect our ministry.

WHY PARENTS BLAME AND WHAT WE CAN DO

When something negative happens to our teenagers, most parents' fears are caused by experiencing a loss of control in an ambiguous situation or complex instability. For people who struggle with obsessive compulsive disorder, a lack of control, chaos, or instability are extremely frightening. But even for the average parent of teenagers fear, anxiety, and imagination can easily get a tight grip. When something bad happens to their kids, especially in church, parents often need to blame someone. I offer this just as a point of understanding and compassion for parents. As youth workers we have to understand that more is going on a parent's mind and heart than what we can see.

In our youth group, some of our most gifted volunteers are teachers in schools. We have quite a few in our youth ministry. I enjoy our conversations, especially when it centers around these teachers' relationships with parents of students they teach at school. Teachers share with me in raw, deep, and difficult ways their struggles with parents when students aren't achieving as well as they could. Parents often have a tough time in these situations and blame teachers for not doing a good enough job or not contacting them sooner. They blame teachers because they are supposedly too strict or not nice enough with their teens. They will accuse the school and these teachers of not having enough options and programs to help their teens.

When I hear this, I see in these parents what I see in the parents of our youth ministries and churches. Parents in a state of fear and chaos are not always looking for solutions but a place to put their blame. It saddens me, but really it's just another reason for me to be more compassionate and empathetic toward these parents. I need to understand their hearts and know it's not actually personal but is instead the difficult outward manifestation of an internal conflict that could involve guilt, denial, or even regret.

Being proactively available to parents has been an effective way to work with them when difficult situation arise. I'm certainly glad I have younger interns who I can reach out to when problems have arisen in my life with my teenagers, and I have actively told parents that if they ever have any issues or problems with their teens, to remember that we are here for them. It's not fool proof, but parents knowing we have been and are always available to help and serve, has curtailed some of the need to blame.

WORKING THROUGH BLAME PROACTIVELY

Blame in the form of criticism can be hard to deal with. Not to belabor the point but, again, if a teenager doesn't like the youth group, parents sometimes can "gossip" and find ways to blame the youth ministry and youth pastor. They can say youth workers are not in their office enough. They can say youth workers need to be out visiting students more. Even the most brilliant youth worker, like our seminary interns, can or will be critiqued or blamed even before starting their jobs, just for being young and new. But when my kids got old enough for youth group, I was given a glimpse of the other side.

Sending my teenager off to a mission trip for a week as a parent and not a youth pastor was very different. I didn't have control. I didn't have final oversight. I didn't have the final responsibility for the trip. I had to trust the others in the youth group, including the volunteers and seminary interns. Now as a parent in this situation, I was concerned they were not preparing ahead of time. (As the supervisor of seminary interns, if I ever feel like the team isn't prepared, I simply have an opportunity to come alongside.) As a parent, I worried that not enough snacks had been purchased and that my teenager was going to starve. (As the leader, if interns are not purchasing enough snacks for the students, I just tell them to get more.) As a parent, when the mission team was leaving thirty minutes late for the trip, I wondered if it was an indicator that the interns lacked the skills to lead and discipline our teens. (As the leader of the youth group, I can always just tell the team to hustle.)

I simply see things differently as a youth pastor versus being a parent, especially when it comes to other youth leaders and the youth ministry itself. I don't always know if it's warranted or not, but it's just the reality. I often hear many youth workers talking about the hardship and blame they get from parents, and there are certainly unfair expectations and critiques. Many parents want too much from youth ministry and workers. At the same time, I also tell youth pastors to seek to understand the minds of parents, especially if they haven't been at their church that long. We need to earn credibility and the trust of parents.

I like the TV show *Suits*, and I remember an episode were the young associate lawyer was ribbing his mentor for being a little late for work and coming and going as he pleased to work.[27] The mentor, who was a senior lawyer and partner in the firm, noted that he'd worked hard for years to earn trust and respect so that no one would question him coming and going as he pleased. He'd worked hard so that no one could say anything, even when he was late now—they couldn't touch him, because he'd earned it.

In the Korean culture, there is this word *injung*. It has no accurate English translation but some would translate it as "credibility" or "trust." It's similar to earning the trust of others. With parents, the need to earn trust—*injung*—is important and it takes time. The stereotypical young youth pastor might be hip and fun, but if she or he comes to church dressed like one of the teenagers, it will take time for the parents to trust the youth pastor. If he or she shows up late to youth group, doesn't seem prepared, or doesn't take the time to greet parents with something more than a "What's up?" the parents may (and will) lack confidence in the youth pastor.

Critique or blame—or even simply concern for the youth ministry and youth worker—is just part of the ministry. Youth workers would do well to embrace it. In order to work alongside parents, we must earn their trust. I'll get to this in the last chapter, but when parents trust you, they can be your strongest advocates, helpers, and defenders. Young Life has a famous phrase: "Earn the right to be heard." With parents, I think it's more like, "Earn the right not to be *blamed* but *trusted*."

CHAPTER 8
PARENTS ARE BUSY

Leisure time is so limited we often spend it on ourselves.
—Christine Skoutelas

The world of parents doesn't revolve around the youth ministry and church. As parents, we are occupied not only with our personal lives, but with managing our teenagers' educational and personal lives. Youth workers need to understand parents' hectic worlds and how the church and youth ministry can work with their busyness.

I think all of us as youth workers have experienced preparing for an exciting event where we can love and serve our teenagers, then our students didn't show up because their parents didn't feel like taking them or they were just too busy. Or what about those times when a parent tells her teenager to stay home and study for a big test instead of attending youth group. Other times, parents can easily prioritize sports or a school activity over going to church. (Many youth workers believe that youth and kids sports are ruining church attendance, as well as the spiritual lives of teenagers.) For teenagers, it seems like school activities often keep them from youth group. Even my youngest son—who is a middle schooler—has school band, National Junior Honor Society, sports, and other things that have conflicted with church attendance.

Ultimately, I've come to realize that the world of parents doesn't revolve around youth ministry and church. Recognizing the parents' busy world and how the church and youth ministry are only part of it—rather than the center of it—is important for youth ministries and churches to understand.

Personally, I value and appreciate parents who have multiple children and have to juggle the lives of their kids. Typically, this juggling rarely includes much of their own interests. In my job, I am extremely busy. My wife is extremely busy. She was once a homemaker, and that is one of the busiest jobs ever. But now she is a professor and counselor. She works by appointment, so one of her tasks is to coordinate her work with my work and our teenagers' lives—there often isn't time for much else.

UNDERSTANDING PARENTAL PRIORITIES

Recently, I read online that when couples become parents, they often don't want to hang out with others anymore.[28] This *Huffington Post* article talked about how hard it is for nonparents to understand parents. It was even humorous for the writer to note that before having her own kids, she felt like parents with children were "such ass----s" who didn't "give a s--t" about their friends. Sure enough, when she and her husband—who'd complained about being abandoned by their couple friends—had kids of their own, they understood. These new parents listed a few points of realization for others without kids, including that schedules for younger children are vital. The basic needs of eating, sleeping, and pooping are vital to the health of kids, which subsequently puts parents on a schedule that is regimented and focused around their children.

The author went on to explain that hanging out with their own children is also a priority for parents, so spending time with friends becomes a non-essential. Household chores, like laundry and cooking, are also magnified. The small amount of time parents of little ones have off, they just needed to relax and have some leisure time for themselves.

As I said all along, I think raising teenagers is extremely hard as well—for me, it's even harder than when my kids were little.

So, I have reflected on this article in the context of teenagers in the church. Even for me as a parent who is the youth pastor, getting my teenagers to midweek youth group activities is challenging. As youth workers, we are competing with family time among all the other things parents need to do with and for their teenagers.

In addition, I still have to feed my teenagers. Perhaps more with boys than girls, but we also have to do their laundry because they smell bad. We have to make sure they get sleep. We sometimes have to remind them to shower. We have to make sure they do their homework and study as needed for tests and quizzes. We have their school activities to consider. Until they get their driver's licenses, and even after, we have to consider driving them to places, especially as it relates to their social lives. In high school and middle school, we have to purchase things for school parties and projects (which they often seem to tell us at the last minute). Finally, we have to fight for home and family time while competing with such things as their social media and tech time and their friends. And often teens go through phases where they seemingly don't want to hang out with us, thus getting them to make space for time with us is a challenge. So understanding parents of teens in terms of church and youth group involves remembering the following:

1. IT ISN'T EASY TO GET TO CHURCH.
Many parents are busy for one reason or another. Some even work on Sundays, and some have little leisure time. I have come to understand that getting to church just isn't a priority or can't be a priority for many parents. It's difficult, again, for one reason or another. This doesn't make the parents bad or evil. It just means they have other priorities.

2. SOMETIMES WE HAVE TO STAND UP FOR BETTER PRIORITIES.

A busy schedule because a parent works hard to put food on the table is one matter. A busy schedule because a teenager is over-involved in extracurricular sports, music lessons, and other intense time commitments is another. One thing parents rarely see is what Chap Clark noted in his book *Hurt*. He stated that "many adults will highlight these and other activities as proof of their commitment to the young ... [Parents] have evolved to the point where we believe driving is support, being active is love, and providing any and every opportunity is selfless nurture."[29]

I know parents are busy and they do so much for their children. I want to understand and respect their busyness, even if they can't come to church. However, as a youth pastor, I've come to understand the danger of a parenting mind-set that confuses things like driving and active schedules with love and care, and I do speak to parents about it. Parents are in many ways abandoning their teens by living this kind of lifestyle, and it's detrimental to their teenagers.

3. WE CAN MAKE THINGS EASIER FOR BUSY PARENTS.

There are lots of youth pastor stereotypes, one of which is that we are not strong administratively. Many of us stink at administration. But when it comes to the time of the busy parents of teenagers, I think professionalism is of great importance. When youth ministries begin and end their events on time, when drop-off and pick-up times are reliable (as best as we can), when the youth group sticks to meeting schedules and doesn't cancel things at the last minute, all these things help busy parents. They will know that they can rely on the youth ministry and youth pastor to honor their time as well as their teenagers' busy schedule.

A few summers ago, two students had high school golf practice late in the afternoon every Sunday, just a half hour after our mission trip preparation meetings ended, and the parents were ultimately hesitant to send their teenagers on the mission trip because of it. The timing was really a challenge, and they were worried our meetings would conflict with these golf practices. It's important to note that these parents saw golf as a way for their teenagers to get into college. So, the mother came to talk to me a few weeks before the sign up period. She expressed the difficulty of the time crunch as well as the potential importance of golf for her teenagers' future education and college scholarships. She also shared that her teens really did want to go fix homes with the youth group.

It has been two summers since, and these teenagers have been doing golf and still fixing homes with our youth group on mission trips each summer. This is because I give both them and their parents a schedule of our meetings months in advance. They can consider their teenagers' golf schedule and plan accordingly. Being reasonable and professional about honoring other people's time has been extremely vital in working with parents and their teens.

4. BE CREATIVE WHEN SCHEDULING YOUTH GROUP ACTIVITIES.

When planning our weekly or even our annual calendar, I try to understand our parents and consider scheduling tactics that might benefit them. Of course, we can't please everyone, but we do *what* we can *when* we can.

For example, we try to leave for retreats on Sundays, when many parents are coming to church anyway. And often we return on midweek program nights because parents would be coming to get their kids anyway. In the summer time, I have to

107

always remember that most parents still work during the day Monday through Friday while their teenagers are on vacation. Hence, scheduling middle school activities during the day is not accommodating to parents. Intentional consideration is even taken to schedule church events after rush-hour traffic. As a parent, I have never understood youth ministries who schedule arrival times to events around 5:00 p.m. That's during the heart of rush hour and, even in smaller suburban communities, there's often traffic.

Other creative scheduling we have tried is coupling youth group events with some potential leisure time for parents. Our midweek program from 7:30 p.m. to 9:30 p.m. allows parents to drop off their teenagers and then go out for dinner or take time to relax. Even sending a teenager to a one-week camp or mission trip with the youth group can be thought of (with tongue in cheek) as a "vacation from your kids." And, yes, it's somewhat silly, but saying it in the right moment gives certain parents the invitation they need to embrace a bit more leisure time when their teenagers are away.

Our youth group adult leadership was comforted by a recent blog post written by Saddleback Church's student ministries pastor, Kurt Johnston. He wrote about different kinds of student leadership in youth groups and the organization and policies that youth groups would require of student leaders, and he shared three models.[30] The first was where leadership was organized with some sort of student covenants and requirements in place. The second model was where it was organized but with some laxity of attendance and other requirements, depending on certain events or times of the year. Finally, the third model was where student leadership was more organic and developed as youth group events emerged, without a formal leadership program.

For our church, we are probably moving away from the first model and towards the second one. Our youth group leadership used to be more organized, especially as far as student leadership attendance, sign-ups, and requirements. But as students and parents have gotten busier, having students attend everything became unrealistic. We have begun to understand the circumstances of parents and their busy schedules. Don't get me wrong. We still encourage student leadership attendance and sign-ups, but we have become more flexible.

Our youth group has also become even more intentional about our schedule in terms of holidays and the calendar in general. We try to consider holidays and vacations in how we respect family time. We cancel or shorten meetings on Mother's Day or Memorial Day weekends. We plan and advertise our youth group schedule, meetings, activities, and mission trips twelve months in advance, so parents can plan for our future youth group events, especially around their vacations and school holidays. This has really helped parents and students attend and commit to youth group events. Likewise, we do send out emails, flyers, and mailings regularly to remind parents of upcoming events.

CONCLUSION

When one of my sons was about to go on a mission trip without me as his leader—for the first time, I might add—he came to me a few weeks before the mission trip and said, "Take me to church. I have a meeting." Although I do oversee the youth ministry and was overseeing the planning of the trip, I had forgotten about the meeting. In a moment of confusion, I'd thought the interns had rescheduled something without telling me as a parent (and the youth pastor). Sure enough, as I looked at the schedule, I realized that as a parent, I'd simply overlooked the meeting time and date. Even as their youth pastor, keeping track of my teenagers' schedules is hard. Thus, it made me realize that for most parents (who are not the youth pastor), it is very likely even harder.

CHAPTER 9
PARENTS NEED LOVE

Probably the only thing worse than the description "family-friendly" is "kid-friendly."

Kid-friendly implies there is no consideration for what an adult may need or want.
—Jim Gaffigan

Ministering to parents within our middle school and high school programs is a huge, intentional shift for any youth ministry. We are often focused on what we can do for our students and don't have time to do more. Jim Burns of HomeWord calls this the "just give me the program mentality," where youth ministries focus on programs while neglecting consideration for parents.[31] And it's not uncommon for many youth ministries, like ours was for years, to be only kid-friendly, with little consideration for parents. However, seeing our seminary interns working with my own teenagers *and* with me as a parent has been a powerful experience. I've seen what it can be like to partner with my interns as a parent, with the interns serving to encourage and enable growth in my relationship with my own teenagers.

So, for this chapter, I've thought about what makes a youth ministry more "parent-friendly." I've considered what parents like me would value and do value as far as the church/youth ministry and have factored those values into some principles and ideals that can be extremely encouraging and empowering for parents.

BE EMPATHETIC
I know, I know, I know ... There are many parents who

would or could be offended by a youth pastor trying to empathize with their parenting struggles if the youth pastor did not have a teen of his or her own. I also firmly believe that there are many parents who would embrace and value any empathy at all. Parenting teens can be a lonely world. Being available and offering to listen can be a powerful and effective way to minister to parents with teenagers. I use this knowledge, understanding that most parents (except those who homeschool) send their teenagers to school during the day, which could provide opportunities to meet with a youth leader during the day over lunch or a coffee break. What an opportunity to give the parents a chance to share and talk about their struggles without their teenagers around. What an opportunity to love teenagers by loving their parents and helping them discuss their lives, and struggles in their brokenness, and how they might grow to be more in love with Jesus.

For me, one particular revelation I've had as I speak to parents who are married or in partnerships is that true difficulties and tensions exist in these relationships—beyond the issues of parenting. And it's something I may not have ever discovered without taking the time to listen and talk to them. I've realized I often need to be empathetic about more than just parenting. Most importantly, I know that ministering to and offering support to parents in these marital and partner relationships is actually benefiting their teenagers as well. Ultimately, parents (like the rest of us) may have issues they need empathy for and help with.

Someone wisely once said it would be unfair to characterize the life of his deceased father by only the darkest memories of him. The same could be true of my father. Likewise, although I have experienced some difficult times with the parents of our youth group students, it wouldn't be fair to judge them by their darkest moments—particularly if I haven't had the opportunity (or taken the opportunity) to know them on a deeper level

112

outside of those interactions.

One last note on empathy: I wanted to talk about empathy in terms of parents and their money. There are those parents who are more financially stable and can pay for all the youth group events, retreats, mission trips, etc. But parenting three teens on a youth pastor's salary has made me more aware of the financial needs of parents and the potential financial toll of involvement in youth group. Hence, my purpose here is just to remind youth pastors and churches to be aware of and empathetic in regard to the financial needs of some families and their teenagers. Just as colleges have need-based financial aid, youth groups would be wise to offer help to those parents who just can't afford all the youth group events. Also, from a parenting perspective, it can be embarrassing to ask. We need to consider these situations and watch for them.

BE GENTLE

A few years ago, I was away in California during the couple of days before we left for our mission trip to Kenya. Since we are working with teenagers, we like to be a little more intentional and thorough in getting ready to depart for these trips. In particular on these overseas trips, we deal with strict baggage weight limits, the transporting of important passports, and usually multiple stops for these international flights. One thing we do is pack all our personal bags and team luggage two days before, bring it all to church, and weigh and label each bag. As we know, teenagers are forgetful even if we announce things to bring a hundred times. And although we had told our students and parents to bring their packed luggage on the specified date, one of our students still forgot.

The leaders who were there decided to call the parents and ask them to come get their son and return with his personal luggage for the trip. When my colleague got off the phone with the father, he called me and told me the father was quite annoyed, first at his son and then at him. The father had started to complain that we didn't explain the luggage situation enough. He was angry that we were even asking him to come get his son at all. He even disagreed with this early packing for overseas trips practice we have been using for years. Ultimately, he vehemently refused to do what we requested.

As youth ministries and churches, we sometimes encounter situations like this. However, near the end of this father's words, he had started lashing out at the youth worker in a verbal tirade filled with expletives. He became loud and obnoxious. He threatened to remove his son from our team just two days before the trip.

My intern confessed to me afterward that his anger built up as he heard the swearing, threats, and abuse from this father. When the father threatened to not send his son, for the first time in five years of ministry my colleague said he lost it and cursed back at the parent. I have to admit, when I got the phone call that night in California about the incident, I was secretly cheering loudly in my mind and heart. But in a sober moment, I did realize that my colleague should have been and needed to be gentler with this father—even when he was facing such harsh words.

Our senior pastor, in working with people for over thirty years in the church he founded, always says some super profound but common-sense phrases like: "Don't stir up the bees." It's his way of saying if you get angry and are too inflexible with people, you'll only agitate them. We *are not* advocating for letting sin persist or being doormats for people to walk all over. However, I take value in understanding his message about angry, agitated people and not stirring them up.

Gentleness can go a long way when dealing with parents,

114

especially angry and hurting parents. No parent in anger needs to be confronted and told what they are doing is wrong in that moment. No parent who has made a mistake with her teenager needs to be told she is a failure or is sinful. Of course, I doubt many of us would ever do so. This is just a reminder of what should be the first thoughts and first words out of our mouths when in difficult situations with parents. I know, personally, that my gentleness will go a long way with them.

BE COMPASSIONATE

My dad died of cancer in 2009. Before his illness, I had no idea—nor did I have any empathy for—what cancer patients and their caretakers face. My dad suffered for a long time as he battled the disease. Together, we visited the hospital at least once a week. While I know it's the toughest for the person with cancer, as the caretaker I also experienced hardships. There was the stress of taking off work, sitting in waiting rooms or bedside with my father, and the fatigue that came from having to take my dad back and forth from the hospital—not to mention the purely emotional toll of a parent's illness.

Today, I find myself visiting members of our church with cancer more often than I did before, even if I don't know them well. I attend more and more funerals of those who have lost parents. I write personal notes of support and care to people who are fighting cancer and the family members caring for them as well. I've had an experience with cancer, and now I'm more compassionate toward others who are affected by it.

Likewise, there is a greater capacity in me now to understand parents who have teenagers. Before my oldest son was a regular varsity starter, I couldn't relate to the parents who lived and died by each play or who cursed out referees for mistakes. But now that my son is becoming quite an accomplished football player, I do see that when it's your own child, you see things differently. Not every youth pastor happens to be a parent. But having a compassionate heart for the struggles and difficulties of raising teens will go a long way as you walk with parents, even if you aren't one. As youth workers, especially if you don't have teens, don't underestimate or dismiss the challenges of parenthood.

BE SLOW TO JUDGMENT

There used to be a mother in our youth group whose teenage son could never wake up for school. She had to get on him every day, which was extra difficult because she had some serious back issues. One day, she asked me if I could call her son at six the following morning to help wake him, but not tell him that she'd asked me to call. She was afraid of making him angry. Now, you probably can already see there were major parent-teen issues going on there, and I knew that too. What really irked me and pervaded my thoughts was how ridiculous and stupid this parent's plan seemed. Even pathetic. How was I supposed to justify a 6:00 a.m. wake-up call without mentioning the mother's request?

I'm sure most youth workers can relate to these sentiments, but as I look back, I would have functioned better in this situation without all my judgments about the mother. It would have helped me love her more and minister to her situation more effectively if I'd stopped criticizing her, even just in my head.

I see the power of my younger interns being non-judgmental in my own life. They are the "youth pastor" to my teenage boys, and I have found it liberating and helpful that when I share my struggles of raising them, these youth workers are there to assist me. They are there to respond to my needs. They are there to work with me as they also minister to my boys. Having youth workers who are nonjudgmental about me has made all the difference for me as a parent as I continue to raise my boys.

BE FULL OF GRACE

Pastors say it all the time. We say we know that God changes people and we don't. As youth pastors and churches, we have to understand that while Christ is in the lives of our students' parents, it takes time for them to grow in faith and to see the fruits of that. Students often tell me how their parents "sin" against them, the wrongs their parents do, the arguments their mom and dads are having, and what bad examples their parents are to them. As a youth ministry veteran, I know there's some truth to the stories about parents, and I take allegations of physical and sexual abuse very seriously. But I've learned to take many other complaints with a grain of salt. I want to embrace parents, and it's important to know that it takes time for them to change and the relationships with their teenagers to change. Still, I realize that many parents aren't growing spiritually and don't know how to grow. They need coaching and help, but are often afraid to ask. I believe it's extremely important for youth workers and churches to see parents in this light—as growing individuals who may long to change. Likewise, giving parents the time and space they need on their faith journeys can be a real point of love and grace for them.

BE AN EQUIPPER

Many youth ministries and churches have the "just give me a program" mentality as noted earlier. We can create tons of fun, interesting, and even profoundly life-changing programs for teenagers. But parents of teenagers need to be equipped too. I often don't see youth ministries offering opportunities for parents to be furnished or trained to love and work with their teenagers. As a youth pastor who is a parent, I'm blessed that I know all the websites and books to read and the seminars at other churches or ministries to attend. However, that isn't the case for most parents. In our youth ministry, even giving a parent a book to read or inviting them to a Walt Mueller seminar has been an eye-opening experience that they usually end up valuing greatly. Parents may not always respond, but intentionally equipping them takes time, so we keep offering.

There are plenty of parents out there who want these opportunities but just aren't given them by their churches. Other times, parents just don't know anything about the youth group and what we have to offer them, and it's just because they don't. It's often no one's fault.

Each summer our youth group goes on a mission trip with Reach Workcamps. I love this ministry, and part of my enjoyment of this trip is that our youth group gets to work with other churches. In addition, I get to meet and work with adult volunteers from other churches. One thing I do each year in meeting and working with these adults is that I never tell them I'm a youth pastor. I do this mostly because I don't want them to feel they need to give me all the leadership of our work group for the week, but this also gives me a chance to talk with other parents in a frank way about the youth ministries in their churches.

One of the parents I met recently was sharing with me about her teenage daughter, so I asked the parent if her daughter was involved in the youth group and if she regularly went on these mission trips. She told me no and that she actually didn't know much about the youth group herself. She only came because they needed another female adult volunteer. As I thought about this, I didn't see this as a deficiency of her youth group. Rather, I just thought that probably a lot of parents are like this and church youth ministries can perhaps do a better job of equipping them with information about what they do and how the staff is available as a resource for parents.

I know many churches that spend energy and funds for youth programs but rarely consider programs and opportunities for parents. I want to encourage youth ministries and youth workers to think intentionally about this. Because I believe many parents would love and embrace parenting resources in a variety of forms. For too long, youth ministry was just about the teenagers. If you're looking for resources that will assist you in equipping parents, there are many out there. Some great places to start are with The Youth Cartel, Fuller Youth Institute, HomeWord, and the Center for Parent/Youth Understanding (CPYU).

CHAPTER 10
PARENTING AND MINISTRY REQUIRE CHANGE

Learning organizations nurture and embrace new ways of doing things.
—From *The Practice of Adaptive Leadership*

Intergenerational ministry is becoming an important buzzword in youth ministry and churches, and of course it is an innovation in the way youth ministry has been done for many decades now. Over the past few years, I have done academic research on church and youth ministry innovation, and I've even been a part of Fuller Youth Institute's Sticky Faith cohort to develop intergenerational ministry in my church. Part of my research has consisted of considering how churches can find ways of working with parents.

Ultimately, with intergenerational ministry, these innovations will be important for the church. In the latter part of this chapter, I'll be expounding on how youth ministries and churches could evolve and innovate as they work with parents—and even what my church and youth ministry is trying to do. Moreover, as a parent of teenagers, these are my hopes and dreams for youth ministry and the church as it moves toward continually working with parents in new and innovative ways.

Most parents have very little clue as to what intergenerational ministry means, let alone how to be a part of it. And perhaps many youth ministries and churches don't comprehend it either. It's true that sometimes parents and churches can treat or dismiss youth group as glorified babysitting. Some parents even value that time away from their teens—not that there's anything wrong with an occasional break, as I've already said.

But lots of churches and parents only like youth ministry for these status quo ways. Hence, intergenerational ministry and innovations for youth ministry must be considered judiciously and launched purposefully.

One of the main reasons for the recent initiatives in intergenerational ministry is a widespread myth that droves of students leave the church after they graduate from the youth group. Fabricated statistics are thrown around like poisonous venom, which has left youth pastors feeling defeated. These erroneous figures typically report that eighty to ninety percent of students leave church after they leave youth group. But other studies related to youth ministry have shown that the statistic of students leaving churches after youth group is being portrayed far too high. Two seminal studies have shown that actually only about forty percent of youth ministry students leave the church after high school.[32] However, one important deterrent to this trend can be intergenerational ministry, with parents playing a bigger role in the lives of their teenagers.

Intergenerational ministry has emerged as a paradigm for youth ministries and churches to nurture the long-term commitment of teenagers to the church and combat the dropout rate of teenagers from churches after they leave youth group. A crucial element of intergenerational ministry is parents being a significant part of the spiritual development of their teenagers. Many studies have shown the importance of parents in the long-term spiritual journeys of their teenagers. Fuller Youth Institute, a leader in the intergenerational ministry movement, calls intergenerational ministry a grassroots movement, and many churches and youth ministries are beginning to see the importance of it. Others in youth ministry call it a fad, some even saying it will fade with time—forgetting that it has its roots in Scripture. Personally, I'm not sure if its popularity will fade, but I think the researched-based rationale and facts behind intergenerational ministry are solid and important for

122

youth ministries to understand, especially as they relate to working with parents and how parents see ministry. Add to that the fact that this ministry model is as old as the church itself, and we have some important things to consider from the parent angle.

For starters, many parents still really like youth ministry the way it is. They like the "separateness" of youth ministry from adult ministry in the church. They see incorporating students into the life of the church as burdensome. More than that, parents who send their teens to youth group do value the youth workers and volunteers and what they have to offer. Hence, there is resistance to change. It's a lot of change for parents (and churches) to process.

Youth ministry has been a separate function in many churches and is not integrated into the main body of the church. There's a strong history behind student ministry that is done this way, hence, youth ministry's strength of consistency over the years in this matter can also be its weakness. Parents often love the way the youth group is working. When there's change toward an intergenerational ministry paradigm, students, the church, and parents frequently resist it.

One of the biggest ways for intergenerational ministry to flourish is to continually educate parents on what intergenerational means. This needs to be clarified and communicated well to them. Similarly, churches of the youth ministries need to be fully supportive. Often, it's the church leadership that parents will go to first if they aren't comfortable as changes toward intergenerational ministry progress. Even at my church, I wonder how much the intergenerational momentum will continue, because parents are still learning to embrace it. However, it seems that in churches where the vision is communicated clearly, with parents actively involved and church leadership on board, there is buy-in of many parents.

I know a good friend and youth pastor whose church moved to an intergenerational paradigm for youth ministry, and it took quite a bit of time to do so. They began by considering it carefully among the church leadership and then had multiple months of focus groups with parents (and students) in their church to process, consider, debate, and refine the vision for it. The process took over a year before it was eventually implemented, yet it was worth the time. The vision for it was clearly communicated, and both parents and the overall church leadership were actively involved in the change process in the end. It takes more than a motivated youth worker to make that kind of change effective.

RECOGNIZING THE DILEMMAS

My hope is that churches and youth ministries would recognize and understand parents better so we can serve our parents well, as it ultimately serves our teenagers. One important implication from my research was that youth pastors need to recognize the dilemmas and situations that parents face.

This was also clearly the rationale for this book. Churches and youth pastors (and church leaders in general) need to look beyond the difficult concept of trying to work with parents and really dig into the barriers and struggles of actually doing it. Rather than being discouraged by the challenges of working with parents, churches and youth pastors have the potential to learn to embrace parents and be innovative in the way they work with them. If they can just deepen their understanding of parents' needs and desires, I believe that effective partnerships between parents and youth ministries are possible. Particularly in intergenerational ministry, recognizing how we intention- ally consider and work with parents is a step toward the greater good of youth ministry and teenagers. This may sound like a D-for-duh point, however the dilemmas and struggles of working with parents and their perspectives of the church's youth ministry are important considerations for youth workers.

Likewise, while my research uncovered youth workers' uncertainties in working with parents right now, it was also clear they're capable of envisioning a stronger future. Youth ministries and churches can frame the future and their impending roles and relationships with parents down the road. We can move away from seeing parents as difficult and disruptive and just peacefully work with them as much as it is within our power to do so. Churches and youth ministries can be equipped to shift towards innovation and implement emerging paradigms for working with parents as they understand parents more profoundly.

BRIDGING THE PARENT MINISTRY GAP

A second implication from my research into the future of working with parents in youth ministry was bridging the gap between former and new paradigms for youth ministry and parents. Again, it's important to note that for churches, adopting new paradigms for youth ministries can be quite difficult. It's important to rethink how churches and youth ministries will work with parents and the potential conflict with those who view the present way of working with parents as fine. Similarly, many churches will resist change and not see the significance in more deeply working with parents.

In the research, various stakeholders in the youth pastors' congregations experienced a sense of "loss." This loss was caused by their desire to return to the former paradigms of youth ministry and parent ministry, when new ways to do ministry to parents was introduced. Other emotions at play during this type of change were anxiety, anger, mourning, and turmoil. All caused barriers to change.

What became evident was that the youth pastors had expressed an early adoption of new ways to do parent/intergenerational ministry and it was developed and practiced. However, at a certain point, the gap between the adoption and those who resisted the new paradigm for parent ministry became apparent. Churches were, unknowingly, adopting an innovation that was causing a disruption. What does this mean for youth workers? They need to bridge a gap between former paradigms of working with parents and new ones. Yes, it's going to be rough ... but vital. And often, parents are going to digest it at a much slower pace.

INNOVATIONS

A third implication from my research is that youth workers, youth ministries, and churches need to become *learning organizations*, which is a business term that indicates a high value on thinking carefully about the way things are done, learning from others, and changing purposefully as needed. The lesson that youth workers and churches can glean from it is that they ought to be continually focusing on learning and assessing strategies for working with parents rather than just prematurely latching onto a program and sticking to it regardless of whether or not it's effective. Hence, youth ministries must continue to learn about parents and their situations and how to work with them as they serve their teenagers.

Organizational leadership expert Peter Senge has noted that learning organizations promote a shared vision where top management ensures implementation and personnel sees the interrelatedness of their roles in the organization.[33] There is collaborative learning, diverse viewpoints are integrated into the organization's decision-making, and empowerment is one of the vital elements. In the context of youth ministry, what does all this mumbo jumbo mean? It means that we have to be more involved and integrated with the church we are in (and its leadership) if we want to promote changes in ministering to and working with parents. Hence, to create positive transformation in organizations, there's great importance put on learning by both individuals and the organizations themselves (youth pastors and churches). And isn't positive transformation one of our great hopes as we work with parents and teenagers?

BOUNDARY-SPANNING LEADERSHIP

Finally, the fourth implication from my research is related to youth pastors' leadership and roles in their churches. The youth pastors in my research described empowered roles for themselves, which were unique and vital leadership positions for developing ministries and working both with parents and within their churches. The impact of these empowered roles was expressed in various ways. For example, the youth pastors saw themselves as leaders who effected change, contributed to the vision of the church, and were shapers for intergenerational and parent ministry initiatives in their churches. The youth pastors also noted that they no longer saw themselves as just the "youth pastors" and that this expanded role was vital for working with parents and in their churches. Their roles now included working more actively with adults, parents, and giving pastoral care not just to teenagers but adults as well. Along with this often came title changes such as family pastor or intergenerational pastor.

Ultimately, the implication for churches and youth pastors working with parents as a new paradigm for youth ministry is that youth pastors can no longer be just "youth pastors." Their roles must be permanently redesigned. Perhaps even just the terminology "youth pastor" must be done away with forever. However, more than that, they must be given boundary-spanning roles to function and work across different ministries, because ministry to parents is, by definition, no longer a youth pastor serving only youth.

In the end, whether it's intergenerational ministry or other innovations, youth ministries will be served well by churches and youth ministries who think about ways to transform, especially in regard to working with parents. However, in working with these parents of teenagers, churches and youth ministries need to consider the perspectives of parents and how to most effectively work with and serve them and their teenagers as best as they can.

CHAPTER 11
PARENTS CAN BE A BLESSING

It is time for us to reject the wholesale cynicism of our culture regarding adolescence. Rather than years of undirected and unproductive struggle, these are years of unprecedented opportunity. They are the golden age of parenting.

—Paul Tripp

I have seen firsthand as a parent and a youth worker that adolescence can be a golden age for parents and a golden age for ministry. In fact, in this relationship between parents and youth ministries, I have found seven key concepts for working with parents in ways that parents can appreciate and value. These concepts provide opportunities to engage parents in their journeys as they partner with youth ministries and churches. These concepts—the Seven Cs—also try to balance parental commitment and provide openness to the diversity of parents that are part of the youth ministry. The seven Cs are Commitment, Co-labor, Counsel, Connection, Communication, Contribution, and Covenant.

THE SEVEN Cs OF WORKING WITH PARENTS

1. COMMITMENT

Youth workers must be committed to the spiritual vision, goals, and values of their youth ministries as they see God directing. They must not only communicate these commitments, but be firm in their dedication to them. Many times, parents may be driven by different values and goals for their teenagers. They may not agree with the philosophy of the youth ministry or what direction it's going. They may feel that students are being taken away from "more important" matters because of the youth group activities and meetings. I noted earlier that a seminary professor of mine once said that a good youth pastor is not popular, and if we commit to effective youth ministry in our churches, we will (at times) not be popular. But we must find our identity in Christ and be faithful to God's vision given to us for our students. When it comes to parents, we must sometimes hold to our committed values and agree to disagree.

One principle I've always believed in is that youth workers are to be "used but not abused"—as in we must allow ourselves to be used by God but not be abused by parents. Youth workers are used by God to promote his agenda and bring it to fruition, and often parents want to help the youth ministry in this goal. However, we must be careful they are promoting what God has called youth workers to and what God wants for the youth ministry. Parents, even with good intentions, may also have some ideas, thoughts, or programs they feel may be "better" for the youth group. (That's how the mind of a parent often works, since they want what they perceive to be the best for their children and often don't realize it may not be good for all.)

Ultimately, while it is wise for youth workers to listen to and pray about any suggestions that parents may have—sometimes they might be right—it's also important to remember our commitment lies with promoting God's visions and ideals and not being manipulated by parents so that they can get what they want out of the ministry.

2. CO-LABOR

One aspect of youth ministry that most youth workers want to promote is the idea that youth ministry starts at home. Ministry and raising teenagers is first and foremost the responsibility of the parents. In that way, youth ministries are co-laborers with the parents. I noted earlier that many youth ministries like to use the terminology "walk alongside" the parents. We must make parents aware of their irreplaceable roles as parents. It's funny but parents often don't take into account that we probably only see their teenagers for two to four hours a week—and that's only if they are very active in church. Hence, my senior pastor and church make sure to promote and advertise that our youth ministry is a ministry that is co-laboring with parents and walking alongside them in their endeavor to raise teenagers who love Jesus, because the reality is that the parents are actually the ones who—day in and day out—must be teaching their teenagers about God.

We do realize, however, that when dealing with teenagers whose parents are not Christians or are not active in church, we cannot initially promote this ideal. Some parents—because of their own beliefs—may never be interested in nurturing a Christian faith in their teens. But for those families who do attend church, we need to intentionally communicate this concept of co-laboring and remember it when seeking to understand parents.

Being co-laborers also means that we are thoroughly promoting our ministry not as a place of babysitting and caretaking of children. Rather, we are making sure that parents, even non-churched parents, see that we are a serious entity working to minister to students' hearts, issues, and problems—a co-laboring ministry that will ultimately lead teenagers to a relationship with Christ that will glorify him long after youth group.

3. COUNSEL
Counseling and conferring with parents is a vital part of youth ministry. I know the parents in our church really value this. Our parents are offered visitations, meetings with the youth pastors, and formal counseling regarding their teenagers. In addition, seminars, discussion groups, and prayer meetings for parents are an integral part of our youth ministry. In this way, we have to potential to help parents better fulfill their duties to love God and others (i.e., their children) and teach their children about

the Lord, according to Deuteronomy 6:4-9; to become more compassionate, kind, forgiving, and each of the other godly characteristics reinforced by Paul in Ephesians 4.

Specific to our church is a system that gives youth pastors the opportunity to visit different small groups of parents to have discussions, seminars, and a question and answer time. We have also brought in respected speakers and pastors to speak to both parents and youth about "teenager stuff." When it comes to formal counseling, we promote that both the parent and student must have counseling sessions together if it's a family matter, while offering individual counseling for issues that parents may have apart from their kids. Finally, the parents are told regularly and consistently that the youth workers (youth pastors) are available for meetings with them concerning any issues they may have.

4. CONNECTION

It's valuable for youth ministries to seek and find common ground with parents so they have a connection to the ministry. Many parents are concerned about education. As such, it's easy for me to ask parents to take a group of students to a campus/college to visit, even if it means a slightly costly overnight trip to another city. In turn, while we are helping parents feel a connection to the ministry via this activity, we are also building relationships with students and helping students grow in their faith. I've seen many other youth ministries connect the youth group and parents in this way as well. For youth groups, the connection may even promote a longer term, post-youth-group faith in the lives of students. This is often a great incentive for parents to let their teenagers participate, however promoting education is clearly something parents value too.

Mission trips and community service activities are first and foremost about serving God and bringing glory to him. However, parents love the fact that teenagers can also highlight these activities on college resumes. Likewise in our local high schools, community service hours are required from middle school to high school. Hence, our church can offer parents the opportunities for their teens to do their hours through the church. The same is true for a student serving on the student leadership team within our ministry. Other activities that parents support include inviting speakers from various workplaces and holding seminars for college and career planning where Christians with various careers speak on the Christian perspective of their work and faith. Finally, for years we have had a senior night. This is a time when our twelfth grade students come and complete college applications, write essays, and just hang out and eat. Parents love this time and we can also have a time to share and pray with students.

5. COMMUNICATION
Communicating with parents in a timely and proactive fashion is a vital part of youth ministry. As a parent of my son's football team, I appreciate the timely emails of the team mom. As a parent of a student in the robotics club, I value knowing the schedule for the meetings. And as a parent of a teenager in the band, I embrace the fact that the band director gives parents a schedule of all the concerts for the entire school year at the beginning of the year. This is how many parents like it.

As noted earlier, we plan and communicate our youth group schedule, meetings, activities, and mission trips twelve months in advance. This allows parents to intentionally plan for our youth group activities. This has really helped parents be committed to things and students to be able to attend youth group events. Likewise, text alerts, emails, fliers, and mailings can all be utilized to remind parents about youth events in the midst of their busy schedules.

I have learned over the years about some obscure but important notes on communicating with parents.

ON RETURNING COMMUNICATION

A former Youth Specialties team member of mine, Dave Ambrose, used to have a tagline at the end of his emails about returning phone calls, voicemails, and emails. I thought it was genius to have this tagline but, even more, he was consistent and faithful to it. In his tagline, he noted he would return voicemails within eight hours and other forms of communication within specific time periods as well. Parents were assured that Dave would get back to them within the time frames he noted. This kind of integrity and faithfulness to one's word is extremely helpful and beneficial to parents. Knowing that they have a youth worker who is reliable has enabled many parents to trust their youth ministry.

ON SCREENING CALLS

For about ten years, I was extremely intentional about not giving out my cell phone number in order to guard my time and my family time. Having parents call one's home often means parents won't bother to leave a message on a family voicemail, especially for unimportant phone calls, which means less messages for you to manage later. Likewise, having a parent wait patiently for me to return his or her call was a good buffer, especially if the parent was angry or upset. But for various reasons, it has become difficult to keep my cell phone number from being disseminated to the church and parents. It's a fact of life. Sometimes they need it. But with caller ID, I do try to screen calls. Frankly with certain parents, I know I have to do this or I'll spend all my time talking to just a few parents for the rest of my life. However, I also needed to be wiser about this screening habit, as I realized again even recently.

One night I left my phone to charge downstairs in the early evening and didn't get back to the phone until later at night. I noticed three phone calls from a particular single mother and figured if she hadn't left a message, it must not have been important. I actually figured she was just calling to vent about her situation at church. She had recently been in conflict with some other church members, and I'd even heard she was going to leave the church. So when I saw these notices without actual messages I was a bit relieved to be off the hook. No message means it's not important, right? No need to get involved.

Lo and behold, I got a text from a fellow youth pastor later, at almost midnight, telling me that this mother's son, our student, was actually in the emergency room about to get his appendix removed. His mom had called me a few times because she was panicking and didn't know who to turn to without a spouse or partner to help her. Fortunately, my colleague went to the hospital and prayed and talked with the mom that night. I went early the next morning after the surgery to console her and see her son. It took some time to convince her that I really didn't have my phone with me when she'd called and to explain why I didn't call back. I did lovingly tell her that leaving a message in the future would be helpful, but I also learned a valuable lesson about screening calls from parents and might not make so many assumptions about these calls in the future.

ON LIVE COMMUNICATION
It's easy for youth pastors to bombard parents with texts and emails. Leaving voice messages are good too, but I often don't listen to mine for days. Hence, I ask my volunteers and pastors to have "live" communication with a parent whenever they can. Talking to someone directly can be extremely important. Especially if you want to

communicate something about the youth ministry or their son or daughter that is important, a text message just won't do.

6. CONTRIBUTION

It's important to get parents involved in ministry. Many parents want to contribute but only in specific ways. In understanding the different and diverse group of parents we have, their time and even their financial situations are kept in mind as we seek contributions and support from parents.

One quick side note is that there are ways in which a parent's involvement can be unhealthy for the youth ministry. We certainly want to promote a healthy way in which they can get involved. However, in being wise and shrewd, there are some parents who want to be ministry vision shapers instead of working under the leadership of the youth workers and youth ministry's appointed leaders. One way we handle this is by working under the philosophy of "at arm's length." It's just a catch phrase for us. We want to have our arms open wide for the parents to feel welcome to contribute and help. However, we don't want them so close that they are breathing down our necks and trying to dictate what goes on in the ministry. It's just a precaution and reminder in understanding how some parents may function.

Our youth group has set a system borrowed from my son's middle school and we've modified it for youth ministry. It's called "Open Doors" and give parents various opportunities (different open doors) to be involved in the youth group.

MINISTRY CAPTAINS

Usually two parents who coordinate with Grade Level Captains (see below) when an event or need arises in the ministry

136

GRADE LEVEL CAPTAINS
Usually one to two parents per grade (seventh to twelfth) who are in charge of contacting the Voluntecring Parents and Contributing Parents of each grade

VOLUNTEERING PARENTS
Parents who can contribute time at events, such as make food or support the ministry as chaperones/shepherds

CONTRIBUTING PARENTS
Parents who may not have as much time on their hands, but can contribute by donating food and financial funding to the youth ministry

PRAYING PARENTS
Parents who commit to pray for the ministry

Overall, having parents who contribute to the ministry in these ways not only equips them to serve God in a useful way, but also keeps in mind the parent and how they may be best suited to contribute. I like how the local schools do this. Likewise, it has been beneficial for our parents who can contribute in different and particular ways.

More recently, I have discovered a website my son's football team uses to get a variety of contributions without burdening parents. It is called SignUpGenius.com and it provides a way for the team to list the individual contributions (like sports drinks and oranges, etc.) they need for the season. I like it not only because how easy it is to gather the sign-ups, but because by showing parents all the team support options (items, quantities, times, dates) it gives moms and dads the opportunity to find a good fit for their schedules and resources.

7. COVENANT
Covenants between parents, youth group ministries, and God

can be a necessary part of effective youth ministry. Within our ministry, we ask parents to make commitments and agreements with the youth, with themselves, and God. We call these ministry covenants. For example, when a student joins our Student Leadership Team (SLT), parents are also required to make a commitment. This includes supporting their children in prayer, making sure that they are in agreement with the SLT requirements asked of each student, and promising to adhere to the parental responsibilities of having their children be part of our SLT. This is a formal covenant. One example of why this is so important is because our student leaders are required to attend a midweek discipleship meeting. Naturally, this conflicts with schoolwork and activities at times. Hence, making sure parents know what is required of their teens before they begin to serve on our SLT is important. Likewise, we have a covenant with parents for mission trips. Similar to SLT requirements, our youth are required to attend mission meetings.

As noted before, parents are busier and students are bombarded with school activities. Again, Kurt Johnston's take on the different types of student leadership teams in youth groups has helped our ministry evolve and work with parents more effectively.[34] Hence, we continually try to consider the context of each student and family. We try to be thoughtful and reflective on how to use covenants wisely and with integrity in our youth ministry.

We had a student play tennis in the fall season but she also wanted to serve on the Student Leadership Team (SLT). So, we adapted our SLT requirements to allow for students to miss midweek meetings during their sports season. Likewise, many of our local schools have their band concerts on the same day as our midweek discipleship meetings. Parents have been thankful and more apt to have their teens participate in activities as the youth group has been gracious and understanding in matters of attendance.

138

CHAPTER 12
PARENTS ARE PRECIOUS

Excellent parents who can find?
They are far more precious than jewels.
The heart of this youth pastor trusts in them.
And youth ministries will have no lack of gain
(because of them).
These parents do youth workers good, and not harm,
All the days of a church's life.
—Proverbs 31:10-12
(from the Danny Kwon Standardized—and very loosely
paraphrased—Version, also known as the DKSV)

Walking into our church's Vacation Bible School for children recently, I saw lots of parents who were serving and volunteering in the children's ministry. In that moment, I realized that our youth ministry has some really great parents. There are those who are selfless volunteers, small group leaders, chaperones, and shepherds. This may not be the case in a lot of churches, but many parents have been a part of our youth ministry for years, standing with our youth and church faithfully. Our youth ministry cannot survive without these parents and neither can I.

In the previous chapters, I've described parents' fears, how parents seem like the enemy at times, the diverse types of parents we encounter, the ways parents blame, the ways they struggle, and how busy they are. I wrote about these things with the intention of promoting a better understanding of parents and, ultimately, to nurture relationships and partnerships with them. In this spirit, I wanted to conclude in this final chapter by celebrating and acknowledging the many parents who have been jewels for me, for our youth ministry, and for our church. And I know other churches are blessed with these kinds of parents too. In considering the hearts and motivations of these parents, and understanding what makes them tick, it's my prayer for other youth workers and churches to have or be able to obtain as many jewels as I have.

WHY PARENTS VOLUNTEER

Parents of teenagers volunteer to serve and help the youth group for many reasons. Sometimes, it's because they actually like the youth pastor. Nurturing relationships with parents and having these relationships can be a factor in gaining effective parent volunteers. It sounds very simple, but I think I have good relationships with parents of our youth group, which aids in recruiting their help.

Another interesting thing I've found is that parents volunteer because their teenagers really love the youth pastor or the youth ministry. Parents are intrigued to know and understand who this youth pastor is that their teenagers like so much or why their teenagers want to go to every youth event at church. In the midst of a parent's curiosity, I get to share the vision and purpose of our youth ministry. This becomes a great way to find those jewel parents who are so influential for the youth group. They see their teens' love for youth group; they want to know more about it. As God gives our ministry the opportunity—and if they subsequently feel called to serve—we have found many parent volunteers this way.

Of course, a youth pastor being liked by parents and teenagers seems a little arbitrary, although these relationships are important. Hence, I believe parents who volunteer because they love students and youth ministry are the best volunteers. This sounds so obvious but youth ministries must seek to find parents who share the vision and passion of the youth ministry. In particular, I sometimes see in parents of teenagers a calling to love their teenagers and other teenagers as well, most likely the peers of their own kids. Moreover, I love these kinds of parents, because I believe they genuinely love all teens like their own teens. In the end, understanding what makes the best and most passionate volunteer parents has helped and served our youth ministry well.

NURTURING OUR PARENT VOLUNTEERS

While I don't use it as the sole motivator for my "jewel parents" who serve our youth ministry, I believe loving those who serve encourages their longevity with the youth group. While some churches can't afford it, I set aside a budget to at least give a modest gift card to every volunteer parent at certain times of the year. Simple thank-you announcements or applauses are valued by parent volunteers as well. We have former students often come back and thank those parents who have been so good to them in past years. Likewise, having youth group students write notes of thanks has also given positive encouragement to parents who are serving. Finally, in understanding parents who have served our youth group for longer periods of time, I also detect that they feel a great sense of nurture and purpose in their roles and know they are being used by God.

On the contrary, when I was a younger youth pastor, I often asked the same parent to bring in the soda every week or asked the same parent to help clean up each week. I can't read minds, but I think in understanding these parents as volunteers, I probably did not love or nurture them as I could, nor do I think they felt valued. And I probably burned them out too.

In loving parents as volunteers, I try to find a good fit for them in our youth ministry. I consider that some may want to be chaperones in our youth ministry while others want to be more like shepherds. Thus, parents value the attempt to find their fit, calling, and purpose in our youth ministry, especially if they want to be physically present at activities and events. In Acts 6:1-4, I'm reminded that the early church required both people who could serve food and meet practical needs as well as those who could teach the Word of God. Likewise, as I consider our wealth of jewels (parents of teenagers in our ministry), we try to love them by finding a fit for them that has value and meaning, according to their gifts and the youth ministry's needs.

It's important to mention again that youth ministries must be clear about their vision and calling in regard to the students, families, and even the volunteers. I've had many parents who have come to volunteer for our youth group, but because we are relationally based and small-group minded, they didn't end up feeling comfortable in those roles. They have become jewels in other ways, such as volunteering to be drivers at events or giving financial donations. Loving parents can encourage love back from parents in return. In addition, understanding that parents have unique gifts to offer the youth ministry has enabled us to find different jewels to shine in different ways.

FINDING JEWELS

As youth workers seek to find those jewel parents, simply asking a parent if they would like to be a volunteer is a first step that's too often overlooked. I know youth ministries need to be wise in this, but I've come to realize there are parents who want to serve but are never asked. A few years ago, I needed to find a volunteer small group leader. I looked around, screened quite a few people, but couldn't find a person. I finally resorted to asking a parent who was very supportive of our ministry but who I thought wanted to stay in the background. She has since become a great volunteer. I admit—and she will proclaim to this day—that she always wanted to serve in this way, but I never asked.

Now for some parents, they have reasons for not serving and never asking to serve in the first place. For some it's fear, especcially the fear of teenagers. Other parents I have recruited say they don't think they know enough about the Bible. Another common reason is lack of time. I look into these reasons because I want to assess which ones are legitimate. I believe the time factor is a legitimate one. However, I can equip volunteers with knowledge of the scriptures. If it's fear based on the unknown—such as stereotypes about working with teens or that they as adults are not hip enough—I can coach parents through that. But parents have many reasons for not wanting to serve the youth group. I, as the youth worker, need to understand that jewels aren't easy to find and some need some polishing and cleaning up to let the jewel gleam. Parents often think they can't become this jewel, but it's our job as youth workers to help them figure out how God's asking them to shine.

Finally, one way I have found jewel parents is to ask parents who are presently serving to help me find more. Who else better to find additional jewel parents than those parents who are currently serving and are excited about the youth group that they serve? Parents who are already invested and feel called to the youth ministry are often very good at finding others like themselves.

It has been a joy to consider the incredible role parents of teenagers can and should have in any youth ministry. It may have sounded weird using the Proverbs 31 verses about a wonderful woman to instead describe the wonderful parents who have served teens in my church, but I can't help but believe they really are jewels. They have the potential to be a vital part of any youth ministry. And, sure, it's corny. But they've been precious jewels to me, and I believe they just might be for you too.

POSTSCRIPT

A major study on recent trends in teenage spirituality offered profound insight concerning youth ministry. The National Study of Youth and Religion (NSYR), conducted from 2001 to 2005, sought to better understand the religious and spiritual lives of American adolescents.[35] One implication from this study was the continual importance of churches and youth ministries in the shaping of spirituality in teenagers. As a parent, and speaking for many parents, I sincerely believe parents value the church and youth ministry and its importance in shaping the lives and spirituality of their teenagers. In my case, as a youth pastor turned parent, turned youth pastor/parent, I have realized that parents are not my enemy. Yes, youth ministry in church contexts—especially when we are working with parents—is not easy. However, turning this around to embrace parents as jewels is a must.

A youth pastor recently emailed me about his struggles with one family. Although the particular teenager involved was one of his most exceptional youth group student leaders, her parents were becoming too difficult. The youth pastor himself wanted to leave his church over the conflicts, and there are stories like this everywhere from youth pastors. However, I've enjoyed my redefined role as pastor of youth and families. Moreover, I now enjoy sitting down with parents over a cup of coffee or dinner and talking about their lives and their experiences raising their teenagers. I love greeting parents on Sundays at church. I pray and hope parents will come to me with their struggles and anxieties. Parents of teenagers are vital servants and jewels of our youth ministries. But, even still, I can acknowledge that working with parents has been the most difficult part of youth ministry for me.

While youth ministry is meaningful, and I've experienced a

145

lot of joy in my twenty-four years of ministering to youth, the work involves much more than I was taught in seminary. And it involves much more than just spending time with students during lock-ins and retreats, and much more than even seeing the wonderful fruit of spiritual growth in students' lives. All my prior training didn't prepare me for youth ministry. All my years as a practitioner and instructor in youth ministry haven't lessened certain struggles that have arisen in the youth ministry and especially in working with the parents of teenagers.

Working with them involves the challenge of attempting to change hearts and minds that are typically fixed in the patterns of their own desires and thoughts. (Aren't we all?) They have fears, they seem like the enemy at times, they are a diverse group, they blame, they struggle, they attack, and they are busy. But in the end, they are just parents who need help, who need grace, who need to be equipped during their years of parenting their teenagers. Understanding these parents is, ultimately, an important and foundational part of ministering to their youth.

NOTES

1. Lisa DaMour, "The Emotional Whiplash of Parenting a Teenager," *New York Times*, July 13, 2014.

2. Madeline Levine, *The Price of Privilege* (New York: HarperCollins, 2006).

3. Amy Chua, *Battle Hymn of the Tiger Mother* (New York: Penguin, 2011).

4. Nancy Gibbs, "The Case Against Over-Parenting," *Time*, November 14, 2009.

5. Amy Tan, *The Joy Luck Club* (New York:Penguin, 1989).

6. Mark Oestreicher, "12 Things I Love About Middle School Ministry," *Why Is Marko* (blog), June 17, 2014, http://whyismarko. com/12-things-i-love-about-middle-school-ministry/.

7. Diana Baumrind, "Effects of Authoritative Parental Control on Child Behavior," *Child Development* 37 (1966): 887-907.

8. Ibid.

9. Ibid.

10. Paul Mussen and E. Mavis Hetherington, eds *Handbook of Child Psychology: Vol. 4. Socialization, Personality, and Social Develop ment* (New York: Wiley, 1983), 1-101.

11. Chua, 2011.

12. Su Yeong Kim, Yijie Wang, Diana Orozco-Lapray, Yishan Shen, and Mohammed Murtuza. "Does 'Tiger Parenting' Exist? Parenting Profiles of Chinese Americans and Adolescent Develop mental Outcomes," *Asian American Journal of Psychology*, Vol. 4, No. 1 (2013): 7-18.

13. Adam McLane, "What Are Teenagers Sharing on Social Media?"*Adam McLane* (blog), January 15, 2014, http:// www.adammclane.com/2014/01/15/what-are-teenagers-sharing-on-social-media/.

14. Sarah Kliff, "Today's Teenagers Are the Best-Behaved Generation on Record," *Vox* (blog), May 25, 2014, http://www.vox. com/2014/5/25/5748178/todays-teenagers-are-the-best-behaved-generation-on-record/.

15. McLane, January 15, 2014.

16. C. S. Lewis, *The Screwtape Letters*, (London: Centenary, 1942).

17. Lesley Leyland Fields, "What We Forgot About Forgiveness," *Christianity Today*, Vol. 58, No. 4, May 2014.

18. Adam McLane, "When Should I Allow My Children to Get a Social Media Account?", *Adam McLane* (blog), June 12, 2014, adammclane.com/2014/06/12/allow-children-get-social-media-account/.

19. "In the Skin of a Lion" (Season 4, Episode 3), *Friday Night Lights*, NBC, November 11, 2009.

20. J. R. R. Tolkien, *Lord of the Rings*, (London: Allen & Unwin, 1954).

21. Doug Fields, "Conflict Resolution in Youth Ministry," *ChurchLeaders.com* (blog), 2011, http://www.churchleaders.com/youth/youth-leaders-how-tos/138104-conflict-resolution-in-youth-ministry.html/.

22. Ken Haugk, *Antagonists in the Church* (Minneapolis, MN: Augsburg, 1988).

23. Sticky Faith is a movement by Fuller Youth Institute based on the ideas in the book *Sticky Faith: Everyday Ideas to Build Lasting Faith in Your Kids* by Kara Powell and Chap Clark (Zondervan, 2011), which is built around the College Transition Project Research.

24. The five adults to one teenager ratio is supported and taught by those promoting the Sticky Faith ideas (http://stickyfaith.org/articles/the-church-sticking-together).

25. Nick Friedman, "Parents Just Don't Understand," *Psychology Today*, July 1, 2014.

26. Jason Good, "The Seven Stages of Parenting," *Huffington Post* (blog), June 10, 2014, http://www.huffingtonpost.com/jason-good/the-7-stages-of-parenting_b_5447541.html/.

27. Inside Track" (Season 1, Episode 3), *Suits*, Universal Cable Productions, July 7, 2011.

28. Christine Skoutelas, "Once We Become Parents We Don't Want to Hang Out With You Anymore (But Not for the Reasons You Think)," *Huffington Post* (blog), May 13, 2014, http://www.huffingtonpost.com/christine-skoutelas/once-we-become-parents-we-dont-want-to-hang-out-with-you-anymore-but-not-for-the-reasons-you-think_b_5270148.html/.

29.   Chap Clark, *Hurt* (Grand Rapids, MI: Baker, 2004), 46.

30.   Kurt Johnston, "Student Leadership: Three Approaches," *Simply Youth Ministry* (blog), May 20, 2014, http://goo.gl/q1DBlp.

31.   Jim Burns and Mike DeVries, *Partnering with Parents in Youth Ministry* (Ventura, CA: Gospel Light, 2003).

32.   George H. Gallup, "The Religiosity Cycle," *Gallup.com* (website), June 4, 2002, http://www.gallup.com/poll/6124/religiosity-cycle.aspx/.

33.   Peter Senge, "Transforming the Practice of Management," *Human Resources Development Quarterly* 1 (1993): 5-32.

34.   Johnston, May 20, 2014.

35.   Christian Smith and Melinda Lundquist Denton, *Soul Searching: The Religious and Spiritual Lives of American Teenagers* (New York: Oxford University Press, 2005).